Top Maui Restaurants 2008

From Thrifty to Four Star

Indispensable Advice from Experts Who Live, Play & Eat on Maui

by James Jacobson
& Molly Jacobson

Praise for Top Maui Restaurants

"We just got home on Friday from an amazing week in Maui and I wanted to tell you that we only ate at restaurants listed in your guide! It was so great because they came with a little 'assurance' that we were not going to be scammed! Your info was invaluable to us and I will definitely hold onto it and make sure I tell everyone I know who is going to Maui to get the newest version. Thanks again for making our trip a wonderful dining experience!"

—Jeani Adams, Anaheim, CA

"Mahalo for your great guide! We've just returned from our fifth trip to the island in five years, and we used our guide for the first time on this trip. What a great time and money saver! It was nice to have some information about places that weren't there last year (Fred's), and places we've been by in the past and hadn't tried before (Joe's). This guide is worth every penny, and I bet you guys have a lot of fun researching it. Let me know if you need a helper - I come from a long line of good eaters!"

—Samantha Mar, Seattle, WA

"Wonderful guide!!! One of the highlights of our trip was trying an Ono sandwich at the Fish House in Pa'ia. Delicious - and I would not have found it otherwise. Thanks so much. I'm planning a trip next January so I'll update as the date gets closer. Wouldn't leave home without it!" —Dorothy Rivett, Lincoln, NE

"Just wanted to let you know that I've been to Maui over 20 times and this is the first time I've bought the guide. It is excellent! I'm recommending it to my friends here and on the mainland." —Mike Dinstell, Moraga, CA

"My husband and I just got back from Maui Saturday and we found your guide to be very informative! I printed the whole guide and punched holes in it and put it in a 3-ring binder and kept it in the Jeep. We tried several of the places listed and found each one to be excellent. However, I do have a comment to make about it . . . you should have recommended that we each get the soufflé at Roy's! I didn't want to share!!! (But I did). Thanks again for an excellent resource. We would have missed out on some great food if not for your guide!" —Melanie and Willie Harrell, Roxie, MS

"My sister Carol and I visited Maui recently with no clue on how to pick restaurants . . . I loved the folksy and down-to-earth reviews, they get right to the quick about each place and what to expect . . . We were trying to watch our pocketbooks a little, too, so it was very helpful in that department . . . I can't recommend it enough." —Susan Theriault, Plainville, CT

"Just a note to thank you for the ***Top Maui Restaurants*** guide. My husband I used it extensively and found some great food - your guide was very helpful. Merry Christmas and Mahalo for the guide - I'll download it again next time we visit." —Gae Sellstedt, Vancouver, BC

"I ordered your guide on-line. It is excellent. We are from Calgary, Alberta and have been to Maui twice but not for over 10 years, so your guide will come in handy when we visit again in April."

—Terry & Susan Winnitoy, Calgary, Alberta

"We have been home for just two weeks and it seems like we were never away. Your Maui guide was very helpful and we all especially enjoyed Buzz's and Cafe O'Lei." —Gene Miranda, Florham Park, NJ

"Thank you so very much . . . ***Top Maui Restaurants*** is very helpful for planning a rehearsal dinner next June. We will be spending a week in Maui, staying at the Four Seasons, celebrating a wedding. Your service has been exceptional. Thank you again!" —Kelly Boldy, Noblesville, IN

Dedication

To my father, Kenneth Jacobson, who taught me the joy of good eating and how to love with a full heart. Those gifts inspire me today, and inspired this book. *Ich liebe dich.*

- James Jacobson

To my aunt, Sandy Lovejoy, who taught me to trust myself and listen deeply. And also to my hanai mother, Rhea Barton, who taught me to feed myself, to set big goals, and to speak my clearest truth. I miss you both, and love you very much. Thank you for everything.

- Molly Jacobson

Finally, we dedicate this book to each other and to our marriage.

Published by:
Maui Media. LLC
www.MauiMedia.com

Top Maui Restaurants 2008 From Thrifty to Four Star
Indispensable Advice from Experts Who Live, Play & Eat on Maui
By James Jacobson and Molly Jacobson

ISBN 978-0-9752631-4-3

 This book is available for bulk purchase by institutions and resellers. For information, call 1-800-675-3290 or contact us through our website at www.mauimedia.com.

We welcome your comments and suggestions. Please address them via email and send them to editor@TopMauiRestaurants.com.

Administrative support by Crystal Linnen
Cover and Text Design by Dan & Darlene Swanson of Van-garde Imagery, Inc.
Authors' Photograph by Michelle Brady

Table of Contents

C

D

F

G

H

I

J

K

L

M

N

O

U

W

A Special Invitation to Our Readers . . .

As you'll see in the Introduction, ***Top Maui Restaurants 2008*** is truly a labor of love. Molly and I have recorded a special telephone message for you, our cherished reader.

Please call, toll-free, **1-800-675-3290**, **extension 8**, to listen to a short message available 24-hours a day. The call is free from any phone in the fifty states.

Warm Aloha,
James Jacobson
Kihei, Maui, Hawaii

Get the Latest Updates to Top Maui Restaurants 2008

The Maui restaurant scene changes overnight, which is why our original online version of ***Top Maui Restaurants*** is updated every month of the year. The book you're holding in your hands is accurate as of publication time, but changes are inevitable.

We have built an online community designed for people who are planning their trip to Maui called **www.TopMauiTips.com**. Every member gets a free copy of the current month's ***Top Maui Restaurants*** (a $19.95 value) included in their membership.

We would like to invite you to get the latest copy of the online guide - with more restaurants and fresher reviews - as our free gift to you for buying this book.

To accept our special invitation just for readers of this book, follow these steps:

Step 1:

Go to this page: **www.TopMauiBook.com**.

Step 2:

Enter the validation code **090807** to claim your gift membership.

Introduction
A Magical Meal on Maui

"I don't 'like' food. I *love* food. If I don't *love it*, I ***don't swallow***."
- Ego, Restaurant Critic, ***Ratatouille***

This book is born of desperate necessity and soul-searing, passionate love. It has taken two years to write, decades to research, and was inspired by a glorious Maui sunset and an unforgettable meal.

The story is so magical and romantic you might not believe it. Even my own mother can hardly believe it happened to me. But everything I'm about to tell you is true. And it could not have happened anyplace else on earth but Maui.

Two years ago Jim and I met on a beach on Maui. With our first glance we were catapulted into an intense love affair. We each gasped a little in recognition of our connection; it felt downright mystical. Our hands took the initiative and reached for each other. As they intertwined for the first time, Jim murmured "Where have you been all my life?" (Yes, he really said that.)

I couldn't answer. I could only stare, a wide-eyed child, then look away at the sky above his head still streaked with my first Maui sunset. The first quarter moon was already bright and two stars popped out as his eyes twinkled.

He asked, "Are you hungry?"

I nodded, my head heavy on my suddenly weak neck. I *was* hungry. I was also struck dumb and a little dizzy. My arms tingled just above the wrist. Was my circulation cut off? But he persisted: "Do you like sushi?"

This snapped me out of my moonstruck state. My head cleared and I spoke crisply, "No, I don't. I *love* sushi. But I have to warn you, I think most of what passes for sushi shouldn't be fed to a stray cat."

Jim smiled and drew me to his side. We turned and faced the distant island of Lana'i, arms wrapped around each other, pulling our quickly beating hearts close together. Watching the sky shift from pink to indigo to velvet, he said, "That's my girl. I knew you'd drift in someday." The waves crashed louder and louder until they were all I heard.

When time started again, Jim took me to my first Maui restaurant.

Following the petite hostess in her silk kimono through a large, lusciously draped room filled with long-haired beauties and a piano player pouring honey-sweet music all over the floor was like walking into my most private dream. We were seated at a table along the rail on the wraparound lanai (porch). Two waiters immediately hustled away for our drinks.

We toasted each other, tinkling our white porcelain cups brimming with warm sake. The miso arrived and we drank the deep, rich, hearty broth straight from the bowl. We told our life stories and held hands in between plates of fish and bowls of rice. Our fingers and our chopsticks cradled the tender pink and yellow and white morsels before delivering them to our tongues, where they quivered a little before giving up their sweet ocean flavors.

Every once in a while I pinched my thigh beneath my napkin. Was this really happening?

We stayed until the pianist had retired, other diners had departed, and the lights were dimmed. As they cleaned and stacked and cleared, the servers brought us cool water, tiny coconut creams, and refreshing green tea, assuring us that we should stay until we were ready to go. It was clear to all of us that magic was happening, and no one wanted to interrupt it.

On the drive back to the beach, heavy perfume from plumeria trees lining Wailea Ike Drive rushed through the open windows. I asked Jim "Is this heaven?"

He smiled and said "I think so." I had never felt so content, relaxed, and beautiful.

After we parted for the night, I called my girlfriends back on the east coast and woke them up one by one. As I giggled and swooned and stammered my way through the story of my first Maui evening, dozens of stars sprang from their places in the black sky above my car and streaked across the ridges of Haleakala in the most glorious meteor shower I'd ever witnessed.

Our ***Top Maui Restaurants*** review guide was conceived on that magical night, but we didn't have an inkling of it yet.

Two months later, firmly established in our new love affair and still discovering the depths of our mutual passion for food, Jim and I were driving by "our" restaurant when we saw a "Now Closed" sign over the door. I was shocked. How could this paragon of fabulous dining, unbelievable ambience, and stellar service have thrown in the towel?

Jim shook his head sadly and a weary expression crossed his face. By this time we had eaten in many of the restaurants reviewed in this guide, and he explained carefully that each one of them - no matter how wonderful - were in imminent danger of closing due to the heavy overhead and high turnover inherent in the Maui restaurant scene.

Restaurants on Maui, he explained, open and close overnight like tropical flowers. For as many superb restaurants as there are now, several times that number had failed since 1990, when he first arrived.

The following week we took a beach walk after breakfast. I noticed a beautiful restaurant practically on the sand and asked him why he hadn't suggested going there for dinner yet. He wrinkled his nose and said "It's not worth it."

I was skeptical, and pressed him. I was hungry for Italian, I said, and I wanted a special night out to celebrate our two-month anniversary. Waiters in formalwear seemed like the perfect touch, and according to several of my guidebooks, it was one of the best restaurants on the island. Jim gave up with an affectionate shrug, and we booked a table for that evening.

To my surprise and growing horror during the meal, Jim was right. I like to focus on the positive, so I won't go into detail here. I will leave it to your imagination until you read the review for yourself on page 212.

After we left I declared "Why didn't anyone warn me?! We just spent over $200 on a meal that wasn't worth half that - at a restaurant I never would have *bothered* with back home in New York!"

The next day we were still talking about it, and the next, and the next.

Watching my consternation grow at the "inaccuracy" and "unreliability" of tourist guides, Jim's author wheels started turning. The problem, he decided, was that I was relying on dining *guides*, not dining *reviews*.

What's the difference? A whole heck of a lot.

Dining Guides, in our opinion, are next to worthless. Primarily descriptive, they are designed to tell you the Who, What, Where, and When of a restaurant. They leave out the essential How and the crucial Why.

A Dining Review, on the other hand, is written by an actual person (or in this case, two persons joined at the hip) with actual opinions and actual (hopefully good) advice. A good review not only tells you *about* the restaurant, it tells you ***whether you should spend your money at that restaurant***.

We noticed that most dining and tourist guides feature restaurant ***guides***, not practical, honest, restaurant ***reviews***. And unfortunately, the few reviews we did find were not written by people who know food.

Jim and I, on the other hand, know food. We both come from food-obsessed families and are excellent home chefs. We've eaten in the best restaurants in America, Europe, and Asia - not once or twice, but repeatedly. We were even obsessed as kids.

My aunt was a restaurant owner and natural foods chef, so I grew up knowing about and eating healthy, organic food prepared to taste absolutely delicious. I started baking at the age of seven, and made all family birthday cakes, including my own. I cooked for my family when my mother returned to work, and I learned firsthand how challenging it can be to focus amidst chaos and infuse love into the food. I also learned how magical food is when you do it right, and how a good meal can pull a fractious bunch together.

Later I lived in Boston and then New York City, where I ate at the best restaurants (not necessarily always the most expensive) and took cooking classes. I've always had friends who loved good food - and my four years in New York City taught me what New Yorkers have known for a long time: food can be the best form of entertainment. Even when I moved to Montana - not known for its high cuisine - I made a point of learning as much as possible about grass-fed beef, local produce, and the wonderfully sweet, wild-tasting huckleberries the bears love almost as much as we do.

Jim's obsession with food started at his grandmother's kitchen table, at age five. He would study her cooking, trying to capture her recipes on paper. She was a high French and German cook who had never written anything down, so his notes (he still has the "recipe book") include "Stir until arm grows tired." and "Pour flour into one of Grandma's hands, two of mine, until it overflows just a little." To this day he speaks in German when he makes us breakfast.

When he started his business consultancy he worked with restaurant owners so he could get complimentary meals (we have a strict anti-comp policy for our guide and have never had a free meal on Maui - much to the chagrin of our accountant). This allowed him to dine at the best restaurants in Washington, DC, where he was born and raised. He has taken cooking classes everywhere he's lived and traveled - including Le Cordon Bleu in Paris - picking up hundreds of techniques, ingredients, and culinary mindsets. He's even studied Ayurvedic Indian cuisine with Mother Teresa's personal chef!

Once he realized the desperate need for a genuinely insightful, useful, honest, advice-oriented Maui restaurant review, Jim suggested we draft a review of "our" two restaurants: the dreamy-but-closed Japanese place and the too-well-marketed-to-die-a-natural-death Italian joint.

And that's how ***Top Maui Restaurants*** guide was born. The more we wrote, the more we wanted to write, until soon we had over fifty reviews. We started selling our guide to people researching their Maui vacation online. We still do. Over the years the guide has increased to over 200 pages in PDF form.

We get mail everyday from readers who have just spent time on Maui and used our guide. Their stories about the memorable meals they've had are touching and spur us to create an even better guide for next month. Our standards for ourselves get higher almost by the day.

Every single month we update the guide: freshening reviews with new impressions from recent visits and noting any major changes to the restaurant scene. Because we update it every month, our readers are guaranteed they are getting the most current, up-to-date evaluation from local foodies in the know. Traditional dining guides have many restaurants listed that no longer exist, and none of the new ones that have sprung up since publication. We get around that publishing *faux pas* with our monthly update. This is one of the most important ways we help visitors plan a really special trip.

Over the years, many people have asked if there was a book version available. They didn't want to print out 200 pages from their home computers. We always shook our head dismissively and said "Who needs another travel book to Maui?"

But the demand kept coming, and we've finally given in. This is, as far as we can tell, the definitive dining review guide to Maui. And because we will still update our online version every month, we will be able to update the book version, too, hopefully every year. We think the demand will keep pace.

Everyone who visits Maui feels the magic that flows through this place. It's not just paradise on earth, not just white sand beaches, endless skies, warm breezes, swaying palm trees, lush rainforests, green volcanoes, whales, dolphins, and rum drinks.

There's something else at work here. We don't want to get too woozy, but Maui can make you kind of . . . woozy. It's so . . . delicious. Like a coconut warm from the sun, cut open and spilling its milk down your throat, it's sweet. When you come here, you relax on some deeper level and life starts looking more manageable. Parts of you that may have been dormant wake up. Life looks . . . good.

We want you to relax on your vacation, and then relax some more. Stressing out about food – about when, where, how much, or what to eat – should not be on your agenda. Let us guide you. We write these reviews as if we were writing to our friends, and we would never recommend a place that we wouldn't send our best friend to.

For the purposes of publishing a book, we've trimmed the number of reviews we usually include in the online version to only the most relevant and useful. This book answers the question "Which Maui restaurants are most essential?"

We've included the very best, from Thrifty to Four Star. In case you think we're always positive, we've also included some ringers and some restaurants that market themselves well enough to attract your attention but are *not worth your time, taste buds, or vacation dollars.*

We take no prisoners when we write. If the place looks dirty, we say so. If the food is overcooked, we point it out. If the dessert is brilliant, we cheer and ooh and ahh. The better the restaurant, the pickier we get. But we don't expect a banana bread stand by the side of the highway to rise to the standards set by Four Star restaurants.

Because we've never published in book form before, we've been reviewing restaurants under the radar and anonymously for years. We don't believe any restaurateurs know who we are, because we've never sold our online review to Maui locals.

We eat out an average of eleven times every week, rotating through restaurants to update our reviews. Over time, we've refined our methods for researching and writing reviews to a science.

When we first visit a restaurant, I excuse myself at least four times to discreetly capture my detailed notes in "private" in a bathroom stall. Jim, meantime, taps away on his PDA, sending emails to himself with his notes. During the meal, we ask lots of questions of the servers, the busboys, and the hostess, trying to pick up as much information as possible about food preparation, the owners, the chef's philosophy, and the way they operate their business. If they ask us why we're so interested, we open our eyes wide and say "Because we love food so much!"

We often tape our "car conversations" immediately after the meal, so we can catch our first joint impressions about the food and the restaurant. We write our first draft of the review as soon as possible.

We return to the restaurant over and over to refine our opinion and keep things "fresh." If we hear about a change in the chef, a new menu, or a renovation, we make a visit to check it out. If a friend or a reader emails us or calls to let us know about a problem, we make a trip to investigate. We have even started an online community to keep a journal and let other Food-Obsessed-Maui-Lovers share their opinions and impressions (information is available at www.TopMauiBook.com).

We eat about six disappointing meals every week to make sure that you don't have to. The result? Well, we've gained some weight, there's no denying. And we've gotten into some full-scale shouting matches that turned out to be nothing more than bad-food-induced temper tantrums. And we've spent a heck of a lot of money on food that would make you cringe, since we don't take complimentary meals (and never will).

Our friends think we're nuts. They're happy to help by dining with us at certain places, and they report their own dining experiences back to us, but they refuse to eat at many of the restaurants we have to review. We just can't convince them to help at, say, H******* in Lahaina. Even if we have to do it alone, we do it.

We have a responsibility to our readers. We have to drink the coffee, and hope it doesn't still taste like burnt beans with a shoe leather finish and then write about it.

Friends shake their heads, confused. But if they happen to work with visitors, they always ask us about our new favorites. Why? Because the number one question they field from visitors is "Where should we eat tonight?"

You won't be asking that question. You'll be spending your time on Maui lazing by the pool, trailing your fingers in the tidal basins, or snorkeling. Thoughts of where to go to dinner may enter your mind, but they'll quickly be answered by flipping through this guide.

At least, that's our hope. After all, Maui can be magic – as our story shows – and we wouldn't want its romance lessened in any way for you, our food-obsessed readers.

We were married on Lana'i not too long ago. One day during our honeymoon, we caught a glimpse of Maui and knew we were looking at the Maui beach on which we met those years ago. We imagined looking back through time at our former selves at that magical moment and embraced as we had then, drawing each other close and feeling each other's hearts beating with the ocean waves. We thought of our home, just one block away from that beach, and sighed with contentment and happiness.

It's our most sincere hope that you will have a magical time while you are on Maui, too. This book should help.

Jim and I wish you shooting stars and glorious sunsets, and very, very good eating.

Warm Aloha,
Molly Jacobson
Kihei, Maui, Hawaii

How to Use This Guide

It may be fairly self-explanatory, but just in case it's not transparent, here are some things to keep in mind.

Ratings

We thought long and hard before we created our restaurant rating system. We wanted to create an easy way for you to glance at the numbers and get an idea of what you are in for.

We think they're useful, but we don't intend them to rule any of your decisions. Some places may score very high on food and very low on ambience, but still are a great deal and a must-visit. We hope you pay more attention to the individual scores than the total score, because we think they're more useful in making decisions. Some places (like coffee shops and ice cream places) don't have ratings associated with them, because we don't think they are necessary.

It's probably easiest for us to just explain each category, so here we go:

Ambience: 25 possible points

This rating tells you what we think about the environment of the restaurant. Generally these ratings will reflect how "nice" a place it is. Beach shacks may score as low as a 5, while Four Star restaurants as high as a 24. Restaurants lose points for dirt, being stuffy in the heat, too windy, or in poor condition, among other reasons.

Food: 25 possible points

This rating reflects how we judge the quality of food and the skill with which it is prepared. Restaurants lose points for commercial food service ingredients (with local produce, beef, and fish plentiful on Maui, we don't think there's much room for second-class ingredients), lousy recipes, unskilled prep work, and over- or under-cooking food.

Service: 25 possible points

This rating reflects how we feel about the service, from phoning for a reservation through saying good night on the way out the door. Restaurants lose points for indifferent or pretentious service (we think each is bad), slow service, and sloppiness or lack of courtesy.

Value: 25 possible points

This rating reflects how good a deal the restaurant represents when we take the previous three scores and the average price of meals into account. A beach shack that quickly serves up bone-sucking good $5 ribs might get a value score of 24, while an expensive restaurant with pretentious service and so-so food might get a value score of 15. Accordingly, an expensive restaurant with stellar service and fabulous food and ambience could easily get a value score of 23.

Total Score: 100 possible points

This is all four categories added together. If you look at the highest ranked restaurants, you will see why our system works: there are restaurants in every price range in the top ranks, because some of the cheaper restaurants have value scores as high as expensive ones. While our favorite restaurants tend to have the highest overall score, we think the four sub-scores are more important when choosing where to eat. And some of our very favorite restaurants actually score lower than we would like them to, usually because of some flaw in ambience or service that we can't truthfully rate higher.

What's most important to recognize is ***everything is relative***. The real value in this scoring system appears only when you compare restaurants to one another.

There *is* a difference between an 86 and an 84, but you will only know what it is by reading the reviews and looking at the sub-scores.

We stand by our opinions, but we recognize that others don't always agree with us. We think of this as a conversation, not a absolute pronouncement, especially since our reviews and ratings can change every month depending on the latest experience. That's why we are so excited about our dynamic online community, where we can all share our perspectives.

Top Picks

If a restaurant stands out in some way, we point it out with a "Top" award. You can find these awards above the reviews and also in the separate listing called **Our Top Picks** on page 41.

Location/Parking/Hours/Websites

Every restaurant has the region of the island listed (see map on page 45) and the actual street address. We also tell you in plain English how to find it once you are in the neighborhood. We tell you where to park, the phone number, and the hours at publication time. If the restaurant has a website, we'll list it.

Meals/Cost

We list the meals served, and also what cuisines and dishes the restaurant is known for. If you have a specific dish in mind, check out our listing called **"Honey, What're You in the Mood For?"** where you will find our best recommendations for restaurants Thrifty to Four Star in each category.

The price ranges listed in reviews represent the cost of entrees only, not sides, drinks, tax, or tip.

Kid-Friendly

Most restaurants on Maui expect to feed your kids (keiki) at some point, and many have separate "keiki" menus. We try to note all of that in this listing.

If you see "Yes," it does not necessarily mean that the place has a keiki menu, but that we have seen children enjoying themselves here. We don't think children should eat hot dogs and chicken fingers for every meal – if yours disagree, make sure you pick a restaurant that has a children's menu listed, or call ahead and see if they do. If a restaurant truly isn't appropriate for children, we leave the listing off.

View

Not every restaurant has a beautiful view – in fact, many don't. We tend to cover the view (or lack of it) in the full reviews, but this listing will give you a heads up about what to expect and what you'll see.

Alcohol

The alcohol policy is outlined. Some places just serve beer and wine, others have a full bar, and some . . . we love this . . . have a BYOB policy. If you decide to bring your own beer or wine, we suggest buying it at Costco (in Kahului) or Long's Drug Stores (various locations throughout the island) for the best value and selection.

Reservations

Most restaurants can accommodate you the same day, although the more expensive the restaurant, the less true this may be. We tell you whether a reservation is Optional, Recommended, or Required. In some cases, we tell you that they aren't available at all. If there is no information about reservations, assume that they are not required.

Credit Cards

The listing "All Major" means that American Express, Discover, MasterCard, and Visa are accepted. The legend for credit cards is as follows:

AX: American Express
DS: Discover
MC: MasterCard
VS: Visa

Accuracy:

All travel information is subject to change at any time, especially information about restaurants on Maui. Restaurants open and close virtually overnight here, and we cannot guarantee that any reviewed in this book will still be open when you arrive. We also cannot guarantee the hours, prices, or menu won't change between now and then. All information is 100% accurate at publication. But for truly accurate, up-to-the-minute restaurant and other Maui travel advice, we suggest you join our online community. You can find more information at **www.TopMauiBook.com**.

"Honey, What're You in the Mood for?"

A Quick Guide to the Best of the Best

We like to pick a restaurant based on our mood, and we figure you do, too. This list includes only our favorites in each category.

Barbecue

Fat Daddy's Smokehouse BBQ
Maui Brewing Company

Boxed/Picnic Lunch

Café Mambo
CJ's Deli & Diner

Breakfast

Big Wave Café
Buns of Maui
Café Kiowai
Café Mambo
Charley's Restaurant and Saloon
Cinnamon Roll Fair
CJ's Deli & Diner
Colleen's at the Cannery

Duo
Five Palms Restaurant
Gazebo
Gian Don's
Grand Dining Room at the Grand Wailea
Kihei Caffe
Longhi's
Marco's Grill & Deli
Moana Bakery & Café
Plantation House
Prince Court
Ruby's
SeaWatch

Brunch

Café Kiowai
Duo
Grand Dining Room at the Grand Wailea
Moana Bakery & Café
Prince Court

Breakfast Buffet

Café Kiowai
Duo
Grand Dining Room at the Grand Wailea
Prince Court

Burgers

Bistro Molokini
Cheeseburger in Paradise
Colleen's at the Cannery
Hula Grill
Five Palms Restaurant

Lulu's
Maui Brewing Company
Moose McGillicuddy's
Mulligan's
Plantation House
Ruby's
SeaWatch
Stella Blues
Tommy Bahama's Tropical Café

Cheese

Café Marc Aurel
Who Cut the Cheese

Chinese

Dragon Dragon Chinese Restaurant

Crepes

Café des Amis

Fajitas

Café Mambo
Fred's Mexican Café

French

Chez Paul Restaurant
Gerard's Restaurant

German

Brigit & Bernard's Garden Café

Hawaiian Regional Cuisine/Pacific Rim

Note: There is a whole school of thought and debate about what constitutes each of these cuisines. Foodies can debate it forever, but if you're hard-pressed to describe each to your friends at home, here's what we say:

Hawaiian Regional Cuisine is a fusion of Hawaiian produce and fish with European sauces and prep techniques.

Pacific Rim is multi-continental and can include techniques and flavors from as far south as Chile and far north as Alaska, with Asian sauces and Polynesian flavors.

We're blessed on Maui to have many great chefs (several of whom originated these cuisines) fluent in one or both cuisines. We don't bother to make a distinction when giving advice about where to dine. Visit at least one of these restaurants in order to sample the amazing fusion that was born here on the islands.

Feast at Lele
Hali'imaile General Store
Humuhumunukunukuapua'a
I'O
Mala an Ocean Tavern
Mama's Fish House
Old Lahaina Lu'au
Pacific'O
Plantation House
Roy's
Sansei Seafood Restaurant & Sushi Bar
SeaWatch
Spago
Tropica

Healthy/Organics

Down to Earth
Flatbread

Hawaiian Moons Natural Foods
Joy's Place
Mala an Ocean Tavern
Mana Foods

Ice Cream

Hula Cookies & Ice Cream
Lappert's
Makawao Sushi and Deli
Ruby's
Tasaka Guri-Guri

Italian

Antonio's
Aroma D'Italia
Caffe Ciao
Capische?
Casanova
Ferraro's Bar e Ristorante
Gian Don's Italian Bistro
Longhi's

Japanese/Sushi

Cascades Grille & Sushi Bar
Hakone
Kobe Japanese Steak House & Sushi Bar
Koiso Sushi Bar
Restaurant Taiko
Sansei Seafood Restaurant & Sushi Bar

Kobe Beef

Bistro Molokini

Duo
Mala an Ocean Tavern

Latin American

Manana Garage

Local

L&L Hawaiian Barbecue
Upcountry Fresh Tamales & Mixed Plate Local Food

Lu'au

Feast at Lele
Old Lahaina Lu'au

Mexican

Cilantro Fresh Mexican Grill
Fred's Mexican Café
Maui Tacos
Upcountry Fresh Tamales & Mixed Plate Local Food

Mediterranean

Café des Amis
Café Mambo
Pita Paradise

Pasta

Antonio's
Aroma D'Italia
Casanova
Ferraro's Bar e Ristorante
Gian Don's Italian Bistro

Longhi's
Marco's Grill & Deli
Matteo's Pizzeria

Pizza

Bistro Molokini
BJ's Chicago Pizzeria
Caffe Ciao
Casanova
Flatbread Company
Matteo's Pizzeria
Shaka

Prepared Foods

Down to Earth
CJ's Deli and Diner
Hawaiian Moons Natural Foods
John Paul Fine Foods
Mana Foods

Ribs

Alexander's Fish & Chips
Fat Daddy's Texas Smokehouse
Gian Don's Italian Bistro
Maui Brewing Company

Salad Bar – Take-Out

Down to Earth
Hawaiian Moons Natural Foods
Mana Foods

Salads

Bistro Molokini
Café Mambo
Café O'Lei
Colleen's at the Cannery
Flatbread Company
Joy's Place
Ma'alaea Grill
Tommy Bahama's Tropical Café

Sandwiches

Ba-Le
Big Wave Cafe
Bistro Molokini
Café Marc Aurel
Café O'Lei
Cheeseburger in Paradise
CJ's Deli & Diner
Hula Grill
John Paul Fine Foods
Joy's Place
Makawao Sushi and Deli
Ma'alaea Grill
Marco's Grill & Deli
Moana Bakery & Café
Moose McGillicuddy's
Mulligan's
Pa'ia Fish Market
Philly's Blue Plate Diner
Plantation House
Ruby's
SeaWatch
Shaka

Stella Blues
Tommy Bahama's Tropical Café
Who Cut the Cheese

Seafood

Alexander's Fish & Chips
Buzz's Wharf
Café O'Lei
Cascades Grille & Sushi Bar
David Paul's Lahaina Grill
Duo
Five Palms Restaurant
Hali'imaile General Store
Humuhumunukunukuapua'a
I'O
Jacques Bistro
Joe's Simply Delicious Food
Lahaina Store Grille & Oyster Bar
Longhi's
Ma'alaea Grill
Ma'alaea Waterfront Restaurant
Mala an Ocean Tavern
Mama's Fish House
Pacific'O
Pa'ia Fish Market
Pineapple Grill
Plantation House
Roy's
SeaWatch
Spago
Tropica

Smoothies

Café des Amis
Down to Earth
Hawaiian Moons
Joy's Place

Snacks and Treats Donuts

Buns of Maui
Café des Amis
Café Mambo
Café Marc Aurel
Cinnamon Roll Fair
Colleen's at the Cannery
Julia's Best Banana Bread
Kihei Caffe
Krispy Kreme
Maui Coffee Roasters
Moana Bakery & Café

Steak/Beef

Big Wave Cafe
Cascades Grille & Sushi Bar
David Paul's Lahaina Grill
Duo
Joe's Simply Delicious Food
Lahaina Store Grille & Oyster Bar
Longhi's
Makawao Steak House
Ma'alaea Grill
Maui Brewing Company
Pineapple Grill
Roy's
Ruth's Chris Steak House
Spago

Tapas

Mala an Ocean Tavern

Thai

Thailand Cuisine

Vietnamese

Ba-Le

A Saigon Café

Wine Bar

Café Marc Aurel

Mala an Ocean Tavern

Our Top Picks

There are a lot of fine eating establishments on Maui, and our job is to ferret out the best.

Below is an admittedly subjective list of our Top Picks for everything from onion rings to romance to dive bars.

Apple Streudel . . . . Moana Bakery & Cafe
Asian Take-Out . . . . Ba-Le
Bistro Grill . . . . David Paul's Lahaina Grill
Breakfast . . . . SeaWatch
Burger and Shake . . . . Ruby's
Chinese . . . . Dragon Dragon Chinese Restaurant
Coffee . . . . Maui Coffee Roasters
Crepe . . . . Cafe des Amis
Crispy Duck . . . . Cafe Mambo
Deep Dish Pizza . . . . BJ's Chicago Pizzeria
Dessert . . . . Roy's
Dive Bar . . . . Life's a Beach
Donut . . . . Krispy Kreme
Fine Dining . . . . Spago
Fish & Chips . . . . Alexander's Fish & Chips
Fish Sandwich . . . . Pa'ia Fish Market
Fish Tacos . . . . Maui Tacos
French . . . . Chez Paul
German . . . . Brigit & Bernard's Garden Cafe
Gourmet Burger . . . . Bistro Molokini
Health Food Store . . . . Mana Foods

Ice Cream . . . . Lappert's
Italian . . . . .Capische?
Japanese Restaurant . . . . Restaurant Taiko
Ka'anapali Restaurant . . . . .Tropica
Kapalua Restaurant . . . . .Plantation House
Kid-Friendly Restaurant . . . . Ruby's
Kihei Lunch . . . . Cafe O'Lei
Kihei Restaurant . . . . Roy's
Kobe Beef . . . . Duo
Lahaina Restaurant . . . . I'O
Lamb . . . . Pineapple Grill
Lamb Pita . . . . Pita Paradise
Late Night Dining . . . . Sansei Seafood Restaurant
Local Food . . . . .L & L Hawaiian Barbecue
Lu'au . . . . Old Lahaina Lu'au
Lu'au Food . . . . Feast at Lele
Ma'alaea Restaurant . . . . Maalaea Waterfront Restaurant
Margarita . . . . Milagros Food Company
Maui Restaurant . . . . .Capische?
Mexican . . . . Cilantro Fresh Mexican Grill
Onion Rings . . . . Cascades Grille & Sushi Bar
Picnic Lunch To-Go . . . . .CJ's Deli & Diner
Pie . . . . David Paul's Lahaina Grill
Pizza . . . . Flatbread
Place for Breakfast After Sunrise on Top of Haleakala or Before You Go to Hana . . . . Moana Bakery & Cafe
Place to Dance . . . . Casanova
Place to Pick Up Groceries . . . . .Mana Foods
Prawns . . . . Buzz's Wharf
Ravioli . . . . Marco's Grill & Deli
Romantic Lahaina View . . . . Lahaina Store Grille & Oyster Bar
Romantic Restaurant . . . . Mama's Fish House
Seafood . . . . Maalaea Waterfront Restaurant

Smoothie . . . . Hawaiian Moons Natural Foods
Spaghetti & Meatballs . . . . Aroma D'Italia
Splurge Restaurant . . . . Mama's Fish House
Steak . . . . Longhi's
Steak House . . . . Makawao Steak House
Sunday Brunch . . . . Grand Dining Room at the Grand Wailea
Sushi . . . . Koiso Sushi Bar
Tapas Bar . . . . .Mala An Ocean Tavern
Thai . . . . Thailand Cuisine
UpCountry Restaurant . . . . Hali'imaile General Store
Vietnamese . . . . .A Saigon Cafe
Waffle Bar . . . . Cafe Kiowai
Wailuku Restaurant . . . . .A Saigon Café
West Side Breakfast . . . . .Gazebo
Wine Bar . . . . Cafe Marc Aurel

Map of Maui

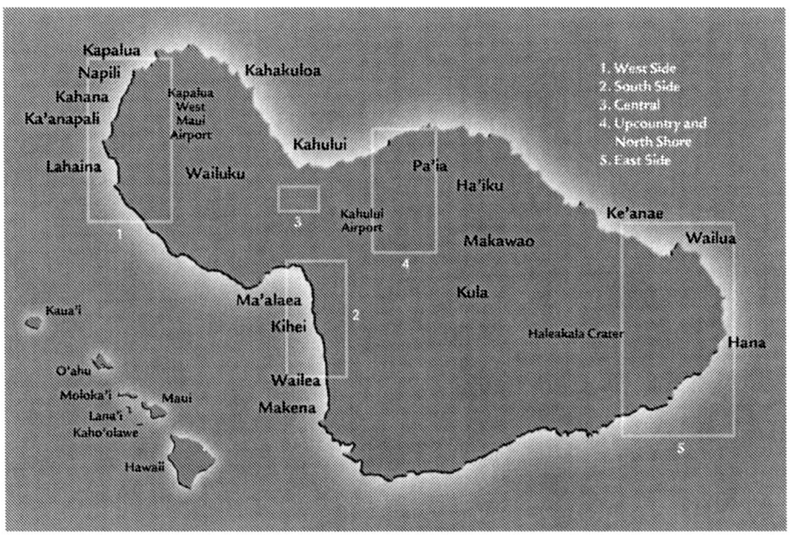

Extensive maps of Maui, along with complete driving directions to each restaurant from wherever you may be staying, can be found on our companion website: **www.TopMauiTips.com**.

You can also download a high-resolution scan of our personal maps marked up with our notes about favorite restaurants.

Go to **www.TopMauiBook.com** to discover the special membership we've designed for readers of this book, and to get your maps.

Maui Restaurants By Location

CENTRAL MAUI RESTAURANTS

Alexander's Fish & Chips
Ba-Le
Brigit & Bernard's Garden Café
Buzz's Wharf
Café Marc Aurel
Down to Earth
Dragon Dragon Chinese Restaurant
Hali'imaile General Store
Hula Cookies & Ice Cream
Krispy Kreme
L & L Hawaiian Barbecue
Ma'alaea Grill
Ma'alaea Waterfront Restaurant
Manana Garage
Marco's Grill & Deli
Maui Community College
Maui Coffee Roasters
Maui Tacos
Ruby's
A Saigon Café
Tasty Crust
Thailand Cuisine

SOUTH MAUI RESTAURANTS

Alexander's Fish & Chips
Antonio's
Aroma D'Italia
Bada Bing!
Ba-Le
Big Wave Café
Bistro Molokini
Café Kiowai
Café O'Lei
Caffe Ciao
Capische?
Cheeseburger Island Style
Cinnamon Roll Fair
Duo
Fat Daddy's Smokehouse BBQ
Ferraro's
Five Palms Restaurant
Fred's Mexican Café
Gian Don's
Grand Wailea Grand Dining Room Sunday Brunch
Hakone
Hawaiian Moons Natural Foods
Humuhumunukunukuapua'a
Joe's
Joy's Place
Kihei Caffe
Koiso Sushi Bar
L & L Hawaiian Barbecue
Lappert's
Life's A Beach
Longhi's
Lulu's

Matteo's Pizzeria
Maui Tacos
Mulligan's On The Blue
Nick's Fishmarket
Peggy Sue's
Philly's Blue Plate Diner
Pita Paradise
Prince Court
Restaurant Taiko
Roy's
Ruth's Chris Steak House
Sansei Seafood Restaurant & Sushi Bar
Sarento's On The Beach
SeaWatch
Shaka
Spago
Stella Blues
Thailand Cuisine
Tommy Bahama's Tropical Café
Who Cut The Cheese

UPCOUNTRY/NORTHSHORE RESTAURANTS

Café Des Amis
Café Mambo
Charley's Restaurant and Saloon
Casanova
Colleen's at the Cannery
Flatbread Company
Honolua Store
Jacques Bistro
John Paul Fine Foods
Makawao Steak House
Makawao Sushi and Deli

Mama's Fish House
Mana Foods
Milagros Food Co.
Moana Bakery & Café
Pa'ia Fish Market
Tutu's
Upcountry Fresh Tamales & Mixed Plate Local Food

WEST MAUI RESTAURANTS

Alexander's Fish & Chips
Ba-Le
BJ's Chicago Pizzeria
Buns of Maui
Cascades Grill & Sushi Bar
Cheeseburger in Paradise
Chez Paul Restaurant
Cilantro Fresh Mexican Grill
CJ's Deli & Diner
David Paul's Lahaina Grill
Feast at Lele
Gazebo
Gerard's Restaurant
Hula Grill
I'O
Julia's Best Banana Bread
Kobe Japanese Steak House & Sushi Bar
L & L Hawaiian Barbecue
Lahaina Store Grille & Oyster Bar
Lappert's
Longhi's
Mala
MALA An Ocean Tavern
Maui Tacos

Moose McGillicuddy's
Mulligan's At The Wharf
Old Lahaina Lu'au
Pacific'O
Pineapple Grill
Plantation House
Roy's
Sansei Seafood Restaurant & Sushi Bar
Son'z
Tropica

Top Fish & Chips

ALEXANDER'S FISH & CHIPS

Ambience: 11 *Food:* 17
Service: 13 *Value:* 20
Overall: 61

The fish and chips meal at this ultra-casual Maui landmark isn't just the best on the island. We think it's the best we've ever had (and one of us is from Boston). At only $7.95, it's a bargain.

At the Kihei location, across from the giant whale in Kalama Park, you'll find a steady stream of families, locals, and very friendly sparrows just waiting for a fumbling finger to drop a piece of luscious, tender fish. Why all the fuss for a takeout window and outdoor seating? The super-secret batter recipe and delicious, freshly made sauces make everything taste "ono" (Hawaiian for delicious).

They cut their fresh fish on site, including mahi-mahi, ono, and of course, ahi. They dredge, dip, and deep-fry everything to your order. Minutes later a plastic basket arrives overflowing with steaming, succulent fish, fries and slaw on the side.

If you're cautious about deep-fried food, anything on the menu can be prepared under the broiler. You can also have calamari, shrimp, oysters, and chicken, all for less than $11. And if you like ribs, try theirs - many locals like them best of all - with the tangy, sweet secret sauce.

It doesn't get better than this for an inexpensive vacation lunch or dinner. Alexander's is a must-visit while you're here, and don't feel bad if you eat here more than once.

Hours: Monday-Saturday 10:30am-9pm; Sunday 10:30am-6pm
Meals: Lunch, Dinner *Cost:* $9-12 *Known for:* Seafood, Chicken, Ribs
Kid-Friendly: Yes *Credit Cards:* VS, MC

Location: South Maui, Kihei 1913 S. Kihei Rd. ***808-874-0788***
How to Find: In Kalama Village, across from the giant whale statue in Kalama Park. ***Parking:*** Kalama Village parking lot

Location: Central Maui, Lahaina
Queen Ka'ahumanu Mall Food Court ***808-877-5566***
How to Find: The mall is at Kahului Beach Rd. and Kaahumanu Ave., anchored by Sears and Macys. ***Parking:*** Mall parking lot

ANTONIO'S

Ambience: 16 ***Food:*** 18
Service: 17 ***Value:*** 16
Overall: 67

Our grandmothers were wonderful creative home cooks and we wouldn't trade them for the world. We would, however, like to adopt the Nonna mentioned on Antonio's menu as our own. Billed as the creator of delicious, well-balanced red sauces, homemade ravioli to die for and Tiramisu that lives up to its original meaning of "carry me up" (to heaven), she must have had it going on. We don't at all mind leaving palm trees behind and stepping into this haven for spicy, comforting, homemade Sicilian.

With a new owner/chef plying the original's tried and true recipes, things have improved markedly in the last year.

The menu is traditional and nods to the many vegetarian locals by pointing out the eligible dishes in the sidebar. With burgers and sandwiches at lunch, pasta anytime, and plenty of entrees at dinner, plus salads and antipasti, anyone can find something to eat here.

Daily specials usually feature a fish, chicken, or steak dish. Recent winners included chicken and artichoke heart pasta in cream sauce, as well as scampi prepared with mussels, shrimp, and clams.

There may be no greater culinary crime than overcooked, stiff calamari that greases your gullet as it slides down. Nonna wouldn't do that to you - the calamari is very good - tender and lightly battered, and the accompanying marinara is just spicy enough to offset the sweet taste of the fish.

The homemade *salsiccia* (sausage) is fantastic. The pasta entrée features their tender, flavorful version over your choice of penne or spaghetti, garnished with green peppers, red peppers, onion, garlic, and a delicious chunky tomato sauce. The hearty portion is served in a deep round bowl with a wide lip, and the bottom shows itself way too soon.

The *ravioli con verdura* is gorgeous homemade pasta stuffed with spinach, garlic, onions, and Gorgonzola and ricotta cheeses. It comes with your choice of tomato, cream, or pink sauces. Go for the creamy pink tomato vodka sauce, a perfect blend of rich cream and acidic tomato.

If you're in the mood for *osso bucco*, this is a good bet. By far the most expensive dish, you'll find the veal tender, the sauce intensely flavored, and the risotto nicely done.

The wine list is adequate, and there are two Italian beers on the menu. If they had a bring-your-own-bottle policy, we would consider this the perfect restaurant. (Long's next door is the best place to buy wine on Maui.)

End your meal with the delicately layered and artfully flavored Tiramisu, and you will be well-prepared to step back out into tropical paradise, ready to take a long walk on a moonlit beach and begin digestion.

Hours: Tuesday-Sunday 11:30am-2pm; Daily for dinner 5-9pm
Meals: Lunch, Dinner ***Cost:*** $9-30 for dinner
Known for: Italian ***Kid-Friendly:*** Yes ***Alcohol:*** Yes, wine and beer
Reservations: Recommended ***Credit Cards:*** VS, MC

Location: South Maui, Kihei 1215 S. Kihei Rd. ***808-875-8800***
How to Find: in the corner of the Long's Shopping Plaza, next to the Birkenstock store. ***Parking:*** Shopping center parking lot

Top Spaghetti & Meatballs
AROMA D'ITALIA

Ambience: 18 ***Food:*** 19
Service: 19 ***Value:*** 19
Overall: 75

We strongly believe that good Italian food makes you happy, wealthy, and wise. Who doesn't like pasta and a plump red wine served by smiling people who love to cook and look forward to feeding you? And who doesn't feel content as a king afterwards?

Unfortunately, finding really good home-cooked Italian on Maui is something of a challenge. Many Americans believe that opening a can of store-bought sauce and dumping it over soggy pasta is "Italian" - and unfortunately, so do some restaurants.

Aroma D'Italia is the exception. This unpretentious, spotlessly clean, checked-table-clothed establishment next to the Kihei Police Station in Foodland Plaza serves good-as-mama-makes freshly prepared food. And they smile while they do it.

We've never had pasta anything other than *al dente*. The red sauce is delicious, well balanced and infused with love. The meatballs are gigantic, tender, and well-flavored. The chicken parmigiana is juicy, lightly breaded, and tasty. The lasagna is loaded with cheese, but with red sauce too. Even the vegetables (served with entrees) are perfectly steamed. The broccoli is bright green and crisp but not bitter, they don't use too much oil, and the seasoning is just enough to bring out the flavor. Mama says "Eat your veggies!" and you do, because they taste so darn good.

This is not *haute cuisine*, but it is solid, very good, homemade cooking. You won't find any surprises on the menu, but you will find just about everything you hope to see. If you are from a city with more than one good Italian place, you might not be impressed - but you won't be disappointed, either.

(Unless you really like garlic bread, which despite every server's claim - "It's the best!" - comes out looking like burnt toast with gritty garlic powder strewn over the top. Unhappily, it tastes that way too.)

The wine list is decent, and you'll find something nice to go with your meal that won't break the bank. You'll also find fun drinks like Italian Sodas made with chocolate syrup, club soda, and whipped cream. Someone back in the kitchen must have had a soda jerk gig to make these drinks so scrumptious.

The strip mall location leaves something (OK, a lot) to be desired. However, there are outdoor seats well-shaded from the sun during the day and fairy-lit at night. The Italian travel prints on the walls, the plastic grapes on the entry table, and the silly rotund-chef salt shakers and lace curtains will make you feel at home. The staff seems happy and genuinely so . . . and if it's your birthday, watch for them to gather to sing *Happy Birthday* in Italian. The music is heavy on the accordion and the downbeat, and between that and the air conditioning, you can easily forget that you're on a Pacific Island.

If you're in the mood for really upscale and romantic Italian, make reservations at Capische? If you're looking for this price range with a more creative menu, go to Antonio's. But if you want to sit down and let Mama feed you, Aroma D'Italia might be your best bet.

Hours: Daily 5-9pm ***Meals:*** Dinner ***Cost:*** $9-23
Known for: Italian ***Kid-Friendly:*** Yes, kid's menu
Alcohol: Beer and wine only
Reservations: Recommended ***Credit Cards:*** All Major

Location: South Maui, Kihei 1881 S. Kihei Rd.. ***808-879-0133***
How to Find: in the Foodland Shopping Center
Parking: in the shopping center

BADA BING!

Ambience: 7 ***Food:*** 6
Service: 6 ***Value:*** 7
Overall: 26

Bada Bing! takes center stage in Kalama Village, and at first it may look like a bargain. Outdoor seating, "home of the $10 bottle of wine" painted on the eaves, and when you take a peek inside you can see lots of old movie posters plastered on the walls and ceilings. The sign promises "New Jersey Italian" complete with East Coast attitude.

Pure marketing. They have (or had) an amazing writer. The menu is filled with funny little stories and upbeat promises . . . unfortunately, nothing is delivered.

The service is disinterested or snotty (depending upon how far they want to take the "Jersey" attitude). The food is worse than bland. It's downright insulting. And the décor that looked so personable at first glance? Step inside to find air conditioning units that drip on tables, stuffing coming out of mismatched upholstered booths and the smell of mildewed dish towels. This is supposed to remind you of a "dive back home" - but unless you love paying a lot of money for nothing back home, why would you do it on Maui?

(We have nothing against dives done right. We'll tell you at the end of this review where else to go in Kalama Village for dives that deserve your business, plus other better eating options in this popular shopping center.)

Sit outside on the Bada Bing! lanai for lunch and you could find yourself in the direct path of a trade wind coming up from Kalama Beach across the street. It carries the beach with it, depositing sand in your hair, drink, and plate. If the food were better, we'd get more upset.

All of that could possibly be forgiven if the food was cheap and reasonably good. But it just isn't. For example, the "Jersey Sub" promises a classic

Italian sub. What's delivered is a slice of ham, a slice of pepperoni, a giant slice of flavorless tomato, and some shredded lettuce on a weak roll so soggy with oil you can't pick it up before it slips out of your grasp. Once you manage it, your fingers sink into the soft, greasy bread and it all falls apart. Add oily fries sprinkled with stiffly flavored parmesan cheese, and you have a perfectly disgusting meal, all for the criminally high price of $14.

The chicken parmesan (which one waitress promised "would not disappoint") is delivered on a super-hot fajita pan without a wooden pallet underneath to modulate the heat. We burn our fingers every time. Mozzarella cheese can hide a lot of culinary sins, which is the first red flag. The dish looks like a sweaty cheese blanket laid over globs of . . . what? Lift the cheese, and you'll find strips of chicken, not cutlets, hulking in their soggy, flavorless breading over a mound of overcooked pasta. Not just overcooked, but actually crispy on the tips of the penne, as if they reheated pasta in a microwave before serving it. The sauce is watery and tastes like they dumped a can of diced tomatoes over the pasta. How much do you pay for this? $17.

And before you get too excited about $10 bottles of wine, don't. That offer doesn't stand. Inside the restaurant all the related marketing has been erased or taken down, and the staff informs us that it "cost too much" to continue that promotion.

If you are in Kalama Village, there are several good options that you should try instead. If you are looking for a dive, go to Life's A Beach. If you have kids in tow and want a dive that won't hurt their young sensibilities, go to Lulu's. Pita Paradise is one of our favorite places for lunch – excellent and inexpensive Mediterranean food. Kihei Caffe does good lunches. Alexander's is the best fish and chips on the island, and Fat Daddy's just opened with some good down home Texas barbecue. If you're committed to Italian, go to Aroma Di Italia in the Foodland Plaza right next door. You'll be greeted by a clean, welcoming restaurant with prices comparable to Bada Bing!, a friendly staff, and old-fashioned-no-surprises-excellently-prepared-delicious-and-comforting Italian cuisine.

Just like we had back in Jersey.

Hours: Daily 11am-10pm ***Meals:*** Breakfast, Lunch, Dinner ***Cost:*** $13-40
Known for: Italian ***Kid-Friendly:*** Yes, separate menu
Alcohol: Yes, full bar ***Credit Cards:*** All Major

Location: South Maui, Kihei 1945 S. Kihei Rd. ***808-879-0188***
How to Find: in Kihei Kalama Village
Parking: Kalama Village parking lot

Top Asian Take-Out

BA-LE

Ambience: 13 ***Food:*** 18
Service: 16 ***Value:*** 21
Overall: 68

Ba-Le means "Paris" in Vietnamese, and the best French bread in Hawaii is made here. We often stop in just to get a few rolls. Meanwhile, the Vietnamese dishes are flavorful and filling.

We like the pho (soup) very much, as well as the noodle dishes; especially the perfectly seasoned grilled sliced pork. The spring rolls are a good bet. The mint is fresh and local, and the sprouts are crunchy. You'll find a long list of sandwiches like ham, roast beef, pâté - all on their yummy bread. None are listed for over $4, and every one gets a vinegary daikon/radish/carrot kind of slaw on the side.

They'll do party platters, too, so if you're traveling with a crowd, this is a very cheap way to feed them with good cold cuts and/or sandwiches.

They offer free delivery on orders over $50. (Delivery is a rarity on the island, much less for free.)

The desserts include bubble drinks (not the best – we'd wait for Chinatown in Honolulu for those) and tapiocas. These sweet and creamy desserts taste like they have too much filler and aren't as good as Thailand Cuisine's (see review), but passable if you're in the mood.

The service is friendly and the price is extremely reasonable for Maui. There are a few seats in their standalone stores, and the mall food courts have tables, but to-go containers are also available.

Hours: Daily, 9am-9pm ***Meals:*** Breakfast, Lunch, Dinner ***Cost:*** $7-$12
Known for: Vietnamese, Sandwiches ***Kid-Friendly:*** Yes
Website: www.ba-le.com ***Credit Cards:*** MC, VS, AX

Location: South Maui, Kihei 225 Piikea Ave. ***808-875-6400***
How to Find: next to Dairy Queen in the Safeway shopping plaza
Parking: Mall parking lot

Location: West Maui, Lahaina 1221 Honoapiilani Highway ***808-661-5566***
How to Find: in Lahaina Cannery Mall ***Parking:*** Mall parking lot

Location: Central Maui, Kahului 270 Dairy Rd. ***808-877-2400***
How to Find: in the food court near the Sports Authority in the Maui Marketplace Mall. ***Parking:*** Mall parking lot

BIG WAVE CAFÉ

Ambience: 16 ***Food:*** 17
Service: 16 ***Value:*** 19
Overall: 68

For good food at great prices, arrive for the early bird special from 5-6:30pm. The deal is buy one entrée get one free, which makes the meal an excellent value rather than a so-so value.

Not that this restaurant is overpriced. Its strip mall location is just not as special as other restaurants in South Maui, so, it suffers in comparison. The food doesn't, however. The coconut shrimp with mango fruit salsa and ginger lilikoi sauce is decadence in a dish. The salt-rubbed prime rib is quite good, juicy and large. The rest of the American fare with Hawaiian sauces is good, too, although nothing to scream about. The fish specials are usually good, and vary every day, so ask your waiter for their recommendation for fish and preparation.

Breakfast and brunch feature a good menu with good prices. The banana macadamia nut pancakes are sweet, rich and filling. They rival The Gazebo's on the West Side for flavor.

The breakfast specials are a really good deal: three different combinations (usually a pancake stack, an eggs/bacon combo, and a waffle) for $5.95. Coffee and juice aren't included, but it's nice to save a few bucks for food that's as good to Kihei Caffe's.

Keiki (kids) are always happy here with a short but tyke-friendly menu. The location in the Long's shopping center is less than luxurious (you have to walk the length of the center to use the public restrooms if you feel the urge), and the open seating facing McDonald's always makes us cringe a little. That said, we enjoy ourselves at this restaurant and recommend it. .

Hours: Daily, 7:30am-9pm ***Meals:*** Breakfast, Lunch, Dinner
Cost: $10-25 for dinner ***Known for:*** Breakfast, Pasta, Sandwiches, Seafood, Steak ***Kid-Friendly:*** Yes ***Alcohol:*** Yes, full bar
Website: www.bigwavecafe.com ***Credit Cards:*** MC, VS

Location: South Maui, Kihei 1215 S. Kihei Rd. ***808-891-8688***
How to Find: in the corner of the Long's Shopping Plaza
Parking: Shopping center parking lot

Top Gourmet Burger

BISTRO MOLOKINI

Ambience: 21 *Food:* 18
Service: 13 *Value:* 16
Overall: 68

Bistro Molokini is the "pool" restaurant at the Grand Wailea Resort. And if you are staying at the Grand and spending a day at their incredible pool(s), we recommend eating at this convenient open air restaurant. You'll pay through the nose, but considering where you are, and assuming that you're spending over $600 on your room, it's a good value (for Maui, for the Grand).

Everything at the Grand Wailea is over the top. Lush flowers spill from balconies overhead and containers at your feet. The entire lobby is open, with very few walls or windows to block your view or the gentle Wailea breezes. Nine Botero sculptures lounge in the spacious lobby, and you might find yourself passing a Warhol or a Picasso on your way to lunch. Placid, blue-tiled water features spread like a liquid carpet, and the grounds are laced with pools and waterfalls all connected by fast-flowing water courses, like you'd find in a water park.

As you make your way through the packed pools (sometimes it reminds us of a paradise version of the Jersey Shore), you'll find yourself approaching a large, open restaurant with a central full bar. The menu features "light" items like Waldorf salad, ahi wraps, fresh snapper on a bed of greens, and Maui onion soup. There are pizzas from their kiawe wood-burning oven, and heartier meals like the Kobe beef burger, rib-eye steak, and baby back ribs. The smoothies (made with ice cream) are truly decadent, and if you want an ounce of rum thrown in, it's "only" $4 more.

During a recent visit, Jim had the Kobe beef burger at $21, "enhanced" with truffle oil and roasted shallots and topped with a slice of Gruyere and fried onion crisps. He was so happy that he ate the entire thing without his normal critic's patter. As Molly struggled with her ahi sashimi wrap (see below) he merely smiled and patted his stomach. A regular burger costs $17 at Bistro, so if you're in the mood, go for the Kobe. It's a great meal at a good price for this supremely satisfying beef.

If you like garlic fries, these are winners: intensely garlicky and flavorful crispy shoestrings. The onion rings, dredged in panko and flash–fried, were thick cuts of sweet Maui onion, crisp and crunchy. Most onion rings look this good, but few taste this delicious.

On this same visit, Molly ordered the seven spice seared ahi wrap. Sashimi-grade ahi, seared and wrapped in a tomato tortilla with fresh, crisp lettuce and salty, crunchy bacon, it looked absolutely gorgeous. The sweet and sour dipping sauce that accompanied it was tangy and light and she dug in with anticipation. Unfortunately, the fish was cut very badly, and a piece of "silver skin" or ligament ran through the entire piece. She couldn't bite through the fish, and instead had to strip the meat off the skin with her teeth. After a few bites, she decided to send it back. Unfortunately it was fifteen minutes before a waiter attended her growingly frantic waves. By this point, she didn't want to order anything else (even though it would have been on the house).

When the manager came over to apologize and fix the bill he assured her that she could have sent it back immediately instead of waiting for Jim to finish his meal.

But that's just the trouble at the Grand. The service is almost universally bad - we think they are chronically understaffed. The meal took nearly forty minutes to arrive in the first place . . . and we had to ask for bread while we waited. The waitress didn't come to check on us until after Jim had finished and Molly had long given up trying to get her attention.

The Four Seasons (just up the road) has service that cannot be beaten on this island, and when you're paying top dollar, you really expect it and deserve it. This is the main reason we can't wholeheartedly recommend restaurants at the Grand, even the superior fish dishes at the main dinner restaurant, Humuhumunukunukuapua'a (see review in this guide). Whatever you do, don't arrive hungry.

Would we make the effort to go to Bistro Molokini for lunch if we weren't reviewing it for visitors? No. It's too slow (a simple lunch usually takes us two hours, from ordering a drink to paying the bill), and it's expensive enough to make us pause. The cheerful resort ambience makes even us locals feel like we're on vacation, but we'd rather go to Ferraro's at the Four Seasons to get a delicious $20 sandwich.

(On the other hand, you could get a hamburger at Bada Bing! for half the price and feel twice the disappointment. Everything is relative.)

If we were staying at the resort, we would enjoy Bistro Molokini for the convenience, and we probably wouldn't really care how long anything took or how much it cost. We'd be too blissed out on all the natural and manmade beauty to do anything but sit back, pat our stomachs, and smile lazily.

And later, get a termé and a massage.

Hours: Daily, 11:30am - 9pm ***Meals:*** Lunch, Dinner
Cost: $20-$40 for entrée and appetizer
Known for: Steak, Kobe Beef, Pizza, Salads, Sandwiches, Burgers
Kid-Friendly: Yes ***View***: Grand Wailea pool, the Pacific, Molokini, Kaho'olawe, and Lana'i ***Alcohol***: Yes, full bar
Website: www.grandwailea.com ***Reservations***: Recommended
Credit Cards: All Major

Location: South Maui, Wailea 3850 Wailea Alanui Dr., in the Grand Wailea ***808-875-1234***
How to Find: near the "adult" pool at the Grand Wailea
Parking: Valet

Top Deep Dish Pizza

BJ'S CHICAGO PIZZERIA

Ambience: 16 ***Food:*** 19
Service: 17 ***Value:*** 18
Overall: 70

Pizza and Chicago go hand in hand - and BJ's Chicago Pizzeria is determined to bring you that famous deep dish experience even though you're 5,000 miles from the Windy City.

Bon Appetit applauds their efforts, naming BJ's "one of the finest pizzas available." This is the only island pizza we'd drive a long way for. That's because we love deep dish - if you're in the mood for excellent thin crust, head to Pa'ia for Flatbread (see review).

Our favorite pizza is called "BJ's Favorite." It's a kitchen sink pizza loaded with homemade meatballs, pepperoni, Italian sausage, mushrooms, green peppers, black olives, and sweet onions. It has just the right heft for Chicago deep dish pizza, and it is as good as anywhere on the mainland. We also like the pastas, and the salads are very good. The full bar serves top-notch tropical drinks and a good selection of brews.

The second floor location above the T-Shirt Factory on Front Street provides unbelievable views of Lahaina Harbor and Lana'i. Sunset is a very good time to visit, especially if you're lucky enough to get a seat on the porch railing. Locals and tourists pack the place to eat, drink, and listen to nightly live music.

BJ's provides a great alternative to the traditional Hawaiian fare served at most restaurants on the island - and few can resist Chicago style deep dish pizza with a Hawaiian sunset on the side.

Hours: Daily 11am-10pm ***Meals:*** Lunch, Dinner ***Cost:*** $12-$25
Known for: Pizza, Pasta, Salad ***Kid-Friendly:*** Yes
View: Stunning. Lana'i, sunset, Lahaina harbor. ***Alcohol***: Yes, full bar

Website: www.bjsbrewhouse.com ***Reservations***: Recommended
Credit Cards: AX, MC, VS

Location: West Maui, Lahaina 730 Front St. ***808-661-0700***
How to Find: Second floor above a t-shirt shop opposite Lahaina harbor
Parking: Street or various public parking lots off Front St.

Top German

BRIGIT & BERNARD'S GARDEN CAFÉ

Ambience: 14 ***Food:*** 18
Service: 16 ***Value:*** 17
Overall: 65

You won't find Garden Café without knowing where to look. This cozy little restaurant is tucked away in the industrial zone amongst fishmongers, body shops, and window glass dealers. This restaurant is very popular with locals, and they focus on lunch and a few evening meals.

But the food is worth poking around for if you're passing through central Maui during lunchtime or in the evening. The little "biergarten" is fenced in and surrounded by fairy lights, so it feels like a European oasis in the middle of industrial gothic.

Mostly German dishes like wiener schnitzel are featured, and we especially like the jaeger schnitzel. There are a lot of daily specials. If it's not on the menu, ask for the pork loin in their hearty port wine sauce. The rack of lamb is another favorite. Skip the desserts, but indulge in the excellent beer selection.

Hours: 11am-2:30pm Monday-Friday, 5-9pm Wednesday-Saturday
Meals: Lunch, Dinner, Catering ***Cost:*** $18-$30
Known for: German ***Alcohol***: Yes, full bar
Reservations: Recommended
Credit Cards: All Major

Location: Central Maui, Kahului 335 Ho'ohana St. ***808-877-6000***
How to Find: On the bend of Ho'ohana St. Turn onto Ho'ohana from either Alamaha or Wakea Avenues, look for the fairy lights.
Parking: Parking lot

BUNS OF MAUI

Ambience: 5 ***Food:*** 20
Service: 18 ***Value:*** 22
Overall: 65

Cinnamon rolls are one of our guiltiest pleasures. Sticky, satisfying doughy, spicy and sweet, they make any breakfast complete.

If we're in Lahaina, we get our fix at Buns of Maui. This little gem is tucked away from Front Street but worth searching out.

Look for a sliding front door papered over with signs that say "Buns of Maui" and "$.08/minute internet access." Inside you'll find a tiny, crowded store filled with random gift items, six computer stations filled with twenty-something girls working on their MySpace pages . . . and a counter that offers breakfast sandwiches, hot dogs, homemade candy, and of course, cinnamon rolls.

Get the version with cream cheese frosting and macadamia nuts and just pretend you're not wearing a bathing suit.

Hours: Daily 7:30am-8:30pm ***Meals:*** Breakfast, Lunch, Dinner
Cost: $10 or less ***Known for:*** Cinnamon Buns, Sandwiches, Breakfast
Kid-Friendly: Yes ***Credit Cards:*** All Major

Location: West Maui, Lahaina 878 Front St. ***808-661-5407***
How to Find: Old Lahaina Shopping Center near KFC
Parking: Shopping center parking lot

Top Prawns

BUZZ'S WHARF

Ambience: 18 ***Food:*** 18
Service: 18 ***Value:*** 18
Overall: 72

Buzz's is a Maui landmark. Located on the wharf in Ma'alaea, they serve delicious food for lunch and dinner every day of the week.

Their seriously delectable prawns are raised in a private farm off the coast of New Caledonia. They are truly amazing: tender, sweet, and nearly as rich as lobster. Any dish featuring the house prawns is guaranteed to be a winner.

Our favorite is the Tahitian preparation. They season and bake the prawns in the shell with a vermouth, dill, and parmesan cheese sauce. The result is a flavor that is both rich and slightly puckery. This preparation is on both the lunch and dinner menus.

Lunch favorites include the fresh ahi steak sandwich. It's simple, fresh, and tender. The Angus beef burgers are especially good, too. We also like the volcano-seared ahi on the appetizer menu.

For dinner, try the Hawaiian teriyaki steak or daily fish special if the prawns don't tempt you. Some folks like the pasta entrees, but we prefer to come here for the fish and leave the carb dishes to other meals at other restaurants.

With its central location, gorgeous views of the harbor, and friendly service, Buzz's is an island standby that's well worth your time and money.

Hours: Daily 11am-9pm ***Meals:*** Lunch, Dinner
Cost: $15-$30 ***Known for:*** Seafood, Steak
Kid-Friendly: Yes ***View***: Ma'alaea Harbor, whales when in season.
Alcohol: Yes, full bar ***Website***: www.buzzswharf.com
Reservations: Recommended ***Credit Cards:*** All Major

Location: Central Maui, Ma'alaea Ma'alaea Harbor ***808-244-5426***
How to Find: Down on the wharf itself, below the Ocean Center
Parking: Parking lot in front of restaurants

Top Crepes
CAFÉ DES AMIS

Ambience: 15 ***Food:*** 18
Service: 18 ***Value:*** 21
Overall: 72

This is the perfect little Pa'ia café, complete with papier mache art and attentive servers who look fresh from windsurfing. Crepes, curries, coffee, and smoothies are made with healthy, fresh, high-quality ingredients at reasonable prices.

The crepes are very, very good, and they come in both savory and sweet versions. Try the super simple cilantro with rice, or the more hearty fresh tuna with potatoes. We also like the brie and avocado with black pepper and apples. We don't sneeze at aioli and tomatoes, spinach with feta, or mushrooms in cream and wine sauce crepes, either.

Of the sweet crepes, the creamy nutella is our favorite. On the other hand, the crepe with Maui cane sugar and lime juice comes in a very close second.

You might not want a crepe when the curry is this good. Served in a huge bowl - you could feed two from one serving - we love the simple presentation and delicious flavors. Try the chicken, it's our favorite.

Salads round out the menu (free crepe with house salad) and are made from the freshest local ingredients. So are the delicious fruit smoothies. This is one of those dining experiences where you can't go wrong. Just pick something that sounds good, because it will be, and at these prices you won't be sorry. And don't neglect to get a cup of coffee - the baristas know what they're doing.

Hours: Daily, 8:30am-8:30pm ***Meals:*** Breakfast, Lunch, Dinner
Cost: $10-$15 ***Known For:*** Crepes, Mediterranean, Curry, Coffee, Smoothies ***Kid-Friendly:*** Yes ***View:*** Baldwin Ave.'s colorful characters
Alcohol: Yes, beer and wine. No Reservations Taken
Credit Cards: MC, VS

Location: North Shore, Pa'ia 42 Baldwin Ave. ***808-579-6323***
How to Find: Right across from Mana Foods
Parking: Street

Top Waffle Bar

CAFÉ KIOWAI

Ambience: 21 ***Food:*** 19
Service: 17 ***Value:*** 16
Overall: 73

The Maui Prince is one of the older resorts on Maui, and its faded beauty can seem dated in comparison to other younger, more glamorous and chic Wailea resorts. But we love the gorgeous, lush courtyard in this hotel with its huge wrap-around koi pond fed by waterfalls and orchids, and we love Café Kiowai by the pond.

The buffet is unimpressive to look at, but under those food service warmers hides some really excellent food. The eggs benedict features a thick ham steak and light and fluffy hollandaise. Make sure you grab some when fresh, because they can get soggy quickly under those warmers.

The handmade waffles are absolutely delicious. They are light, fluffy, and perfectly crunchy on the outside. The toppings are heaped in sometimes mismatched bowls, but are top notch, and you can really work yourself into a fantastic sugar high. Chocolate chips, toasted coconut, macadamia nuts, whipped butter, fresh whipped cream, maple syrup, and coconut syrup are all available.

There is a Japanese breakfast table featuring miso soup, fish, beans, rice, salad, and nato, the incredibly stinky, slimy fermented soy bean paste that is so good for you but a very acquired taste.

For a more American appetite, try their thick and crunchy bacon. The apple mango sausage is sweet and surprisingly tasty, and the scrambled eggs are . . . just buffet scrambled eggs. Look for plenty of cereal, granola, yogurt, and pastries, as well as juices (not fresh - the only place on Maui that serves fresh-squeezed orange juice is Longhi's).

This is a golf resort that also caters to business travelers. Most of the people staying here are fueling up to hit the links or are looking for an uncomplicated, serene background for serious work - hence the many single diners reading newspapers or working quietly on their laptops.

The servers are quiet also, assuming that you have more important things to do than think hard about breakfast. They leave a pitcher of coffee on the table for you so you can serve yourself, and they clear your table when you get up to hit the buffet for another round.

This is not the best breakfast on Maui, but we love the garden setting's uncomplicated serenity, and the waffles. If you're in Wailea or Makena and just want to relax and read at breakfast, this is an excellent choice.

Hours: Daily 6-11am ***Meals:*** Breakfast ***Cost:*** $18-$30
Known For: Breakfast, Brunch, Buffet ***Kid-Friendly:*** Yes.
View: Beautiful gardens and Koi pond ***Alcohol:*** Yes, full bar.
Website: www.princeresortshawaii.com No Reservations Taken
Credit Cards: All Major

Location: South Maui, Makena 5400 Makena Alanui ***808-875-5888***
How to Find: Take Wailea Alanui through Wailea toward La Perouse. Turn right into the Maui Prince Hotel.
Parking: Resort parking lot to the left as you arrive, or valet

Top Crispy Duck
CAFÉ MAMBO

Ambience: 18 ***Food:*** 20
Service: 18 ***Value:*** 22
Overall: 78

Café Mambo's colorful walls, funky mosaic tables, and delicious food makes this a favorite local dining spot. The Cuban décor and Spanish name on the door doesn't predict falafel on the menu – but it's there. So is crispy duck, fajitas, queso fundido (cheese fondue), bruschetta and so much more.

The crispy duck – a French confit preparation that is something close to divine – comes on a plate of greens (salad) or in a fajita form. The fajita is the way to go unless you're really craving those veggies . . . the combination of crackly, sweet, salty duck with salsa, sour cream, and guacamole is particularly delectable.

All fajitas are done especially well at Café Mambo, with fixings all made in-house. The spinach mushroom fajitas are a favorite, as well as the more standard chicken or steak. Mahi mahi is standard on the island, but we'd order the crispy duck – it's a real treat.

The salads are uniformly delicious, with one of the simplest but best house dressings on the island, sweet mango. The hummus pupu platter is the perfect combination of creamy chick peas, lemon, and garlic. Skip the paella – this being Maui, you can get better seafood elsewhere. (Go for the crispy duck.)

Café Mambo serves up thick waffles, fruit, and a great granola-and-yogurt concoction for breakfast. They'll also throw together a tasty picnic to go if you're heading down the highway to Hana.

Drinks are strong and delicious, and they have a nice selection of beer. They also feature Illy coffee, which is a fine Italian import.

PS: Did we mention the crispy duck?

Hours: Daily, 8am-9pm ***Meals:*** Breakfast, Lunch, Dinner
Cost: $10-$20 ***Known For:*** Boxed Lunch, Mediterranean, Spanish, Salads, Fajitas, Coffee ***Kid-Friendly:*** Yes
Alcohol: Yes, beer, wine, and some blended drinks.
Credit Cards: VS

Location: North Shore, Pa'ia 30 Baldwin Ave. ***808-579-8021***
How to Find: Right across from Mana Foods ***Parking:*** Street

---

Top Wine Bar
CAFÉ MARC AUREL

Ambience: 18 ***Food:*** 18
Service: 17 ***Value:*** 18
Overall: 71

Café Marc Aurel is a little oasis of bohemian and urban culture in the heart of Wailuku. Locals and Europeans in the know gather here six days a week for a most un-Maui experience.

The Café is a bistro and coffeehouse until 4pm, at which point it turns into a wine bar. If you find yourself in the area (although unlikely) during the day, you'll be satisfied with their coffee and espressos. The lunch wait staff doesn't know their stuff like the evening staff - so don't be surprised if you get some blank looks. We'd go at night to get the best experience.

The baked items are good, but no great shakes. We'd stick to sandwiches or the cheese and meat platters. Our favorite sandwich is the Margarita, a very simple mozzarella, tomato, and basil sandwich on a crusty baguette. Their hummus sandwich is also delicious.

The meat and cheese platter is a perennial favorite. The cheese keeper arrives to take your order, carrying a heavy tray piled with hunks of creamy goodness from around the world. She carefully describes each one and asks you for your choices. Any questions you have are answered quickly and intelligently. Then she whisks the tray away and returns with a beautiful platter of your selected cheeses plus the cured meats they have available that day. The presentation and the quality are top-notch.

We recommend the excellent apple tart for dessert, although we also like the ice cream coffees. Meanwhile, over 80 hand-picked wines are available for your enjoyment. The servers really know their stuff and can easily help you choose from an excellent list.

There's an extensive entertainment calendar with open mic nights, live jazz, folk, belly dancing . . . and there's always local art up on the walls.

It's rare that we find a taste of real Europe on the island. If you get sick of palm trees and sunsets, you might find the brick walls, wood tables, and fairy lights a welcome change.

Hours: Monday-Saturday, 6:45am-until late, some nights until 2am
Meals: Breakfast, Lunch, Dinner ***Cost:*** $10-$15
Known For: Coffee, Wine, Cheese, Sandwiches ***Kid-Friendly:*** Yes
View: Fairy lights and local art on the walls ***Alcohol:*** Yes, nice wine bar.
Website: www.cafemarcaurel.com No Reservations Taken
Credit Cards: All Major

Location: Central Maui, Wailuku 28 North Market St. ***808-244-0852***
How to Find: Turn right from Main St.
Parking: Street or lot across from Iao Theater.

Top Kihei Lunch
CAFÉ O'LEI

Ambience: 18 *Food:* 17
Service: 16 *Value:* 22
Overall: 73

Whether you arrive in time for dinner or take our suggestion and make this your favorite lunch place - like many locals do - we think you will enjoy Café O'Lei.

At dinner, each entrée comes with a complimentary salad with a truly delicious basil vinaigrette dressing, which makes ordering an appetizer unnecessary.

On the other hand, you can make a full meal from several appetizers if you choose and be very satisfied.

We particularly like the Café O'Lei Tower, with coconut shrimp, tempura, ahi roll, and calamari rings. For entrées, the braised lamb shank with rosemary polenta, roast garlic, and root vegetables is a favorite for its fork tender nature and rich sauce.

We also like the medallions of beef tenderloin with foie gras served in a reduction of cabernet, shallots, and thyme. The handmade buttermilk mashed potatoes are delicious.

The wine selection is nice, but not impressive. The waiters tend to have a generous pour, so ordering a glass of wine or two may be a better value than a bottle. The selection of beers, both on tap and in bottles, is wide, and features some local Hawaiian brews as well as several Japanese beers and wines.

Surprising, and of note (although it wouldn't be of note anywhere else in the world), this restaurant serves decent dinner rolls. For some reason that eludes all but the most skilled of bread bakers, it's difficult to make a good dinner roll on the islands. It has something to do with the atmospheric pressure combined with super clean air (smog makes a good crust, it turns out). Despite all that, you can get good dinner rolls here (we suspect they're par-baked, but that's OK).

Desserts are good, but not especially memorable. Save room for Lappert's ice cream in the strip mall next door. If you're in Kihei and ready for lunch, their killer lunch prices make this the best deal in town.

Hours: Tuesday-Sunday, 10:30am-3pm Lunch, 5-9pm Dinner, closed Mondays ***Meals:*** Lunch, Dinner, Late Night Sushi
Cost: Lunch: $8-$12; Dinner: $18-$25
Known For: Seafood, Sushi, Steak, Sandwiches, Salads
Kid-Friendly: Yes ***Alcohol:*** Yes, full bar.
Website: www.cafeoleirestaurants.com
Reservations: Recommended.
Credit Cards: All Major

Location: South Maui, Kihei 2439 S. Kihei Rd. ***808-891-1368***
How to Find: On second floor - climb stairs up at front of building.
Parking: In Rainbow Mall parking lot.

CAFFE CIAO

Ambience: 20 ***Food:*** 18
Service: 19 ***Value:*** 17
Overall: 74

Caffe Ciao is the best restaurant at the Kea Lani Fairmont Resort. We know some hackles will get raised over that assertion with the much-marketed-but-overpriced Nick's Fishmarket just off the sweeping lobby staircase, but it's our honest, well considered opinion.

Caffe Ciao is next to the "adult" pool at the Kea Lani and across the hall from the Caffe Ciao Deli, their little sister food court. The open-air dining, flagstone floors, crisp white linens and heavyweight utensils aren't just for show – this all contributes to an atmosphere of relaxed chic backed up by attentive service.

The food is simple Italian. Fresh gnocchi is light and puffy, the salads are wonderful and freshly made with good local vegetables, and we love the grilled Panini. Our very favorite, however, is the pizza. A wood-burning oven provides just the right atmosphere for crisp-but-tender crust, and the toppings are first-rate.

You can get gelato, coffee, and lots of upscale delicacies in the Deli, but we'd probably go to Hawaiian Moons in Kihei or Mana Foods in Pa'ia to get the same goodies at decent prices (you can pay $6 for a Lindt bar here that costs $2 at Mana).

Hours: Daily 12-3pm, 5:30-10pm ***Meals:*** Lunch, Dinner ***Cost:*** $25-40
Known For: Italian ***Kid-Friendly:*** Yes ***View:*** Pool and grounds
Alcohol: Full bar ***Website:*** www.fairmont.com/kealani
Reservations: Recommended ***Credit Cards:*** All Major

Location: South Maui, Wailea 4100 Wailea Alanui Dr. ***808-875-4100***
How to Find: Poolside at the Fairmont Kea Lani
Parking: Turn to the left as you enter, park in the open air lot immediately on the left. Or valet.

2008

Four Star

Top Maui Restaurant
Top Italian
CAPISCHE?

Ambience: 24 ***Food:*** 21
Service: 23 ***Value:*** 23
Overall: 91

When we dine at ***Capische?*** we completely forget that we are working and get lost in the sensual experience. When we're not savoring the exquisite food, we're gazing at the expansive view of the horizon and the islands floating in the blue sea. When the sun goes down we're rekindling our romance by gazing into each other's eyes as they reflect the spangly Wailea stars.

When we shake ourselves out of our reverie to make notes, we despair of ever being able to consolidate our thoughts for you. We'll try.

The menu itself is simple and straightforward. On one side you find the appetizers, and on the other the entrees. As a waiter once put it to us, "I stand by this menu. You can pick your order by closing your eyes and pointing." While that is often a red flag for us - a lack of opinion can signal an inability to wholeheartedly recommend something - here it's just the truth.

These confident and attentive waiters will be happy to split any appetizer on two plates and bring them as separate courses. We find this side of the menu has some of the very best dishes, so you might consider doing just that.

We like to start with the Caesar salad, consisting of quarters of romaine lettuce set in a long white rectangle of a plate, topped with shaved parmesan cheese and croutons, drizzled with dressing. The dressing is the real star - a traditional, garlicky, creamy sauce with a shot of balsamic vinegar to pucker it up. We always save some of the delicious homemade roasted garlic rolls to sop up the dressing. The garlic croutons are lightly dusted with parmesan cheese and are actually crunchy - not stale - which requires patience and attention to detail in our climate.

Another favorite is the beef carpaccio braciola. The beef is sliced from the same Snake River Farms filet served as an entrée. It's pounded thin and rolled up with greens, diced onions, and fried capers. The capers are dipped in corn starch and fried in olive oil, rendering them salty and crunchy - so much so that at first taste we thought there was bacon in the dish. A tangy Dijon mustard vinaigrette is served with the beef, and the whole thing plays in your mouth like a fireworks display - the spicy onions and capers spiking over the more mellow and full beef and greens.

(The first time Molly ate this dish, she blushed and couldn't speak for several minutes. When she did, she said, "Either the chef is deeply in love with me, or he is deeply in love with this dish." It was like a scene from *Like Water for Chocolate.*)

Don't hesitate to try the ahi bruschetta, another terrific dish. Perfectly seared ahi reclines on a slice of garlic toast while olives, capers, and a divine truffle aioli tumble onto the plate. It's hard to choose this over the beef, but luckily you don't have to - you can order a "sample" of both for a little less than what you'd pay for each separately.

Other appetizers include a delicious kabocha pumpkin gnocchi bathing in lavender brown butter, quail saltimbocca, and a fresh-as-rain Kula tomato caprese salad.

For entrees you'll find veal scaloppini served three different ways (and you can order small samples of all three on the same plate), a simple-but-excellent Bolognese served with spaghettini, spicy shrimp carbonara, and an exquisite cioppino of spiny lobster tail, shrimp, scallop, clams, fish, and king crab legs.

Our favorite entrée is the aptly named "Meat and Potatoes." A tender, perfectly seared filet from Idaho's famed Snake River Farms is piled on top of a bed of potato gnocchi with broccoli rabe served on the side. Onion jus is ladled over the dish, and the whole thing tastes just like heaven. The gnocchi is light and puffy in texture inside, with a delicious salty sear on the outside. We suspect they do a quick sauté in bacon drippings before plating.

The braised lamb shank with lemon risotto and Maui onion gremolata is delicious, for the most part. Tender and soft, the lamb melts in your mouth . . . but then feels curiously unfinished at the end. We think the gremolata, which features the extra-sweet Maui onions, is just too sugary on it's own for the lamb. We are looking for the more traditional garlicky spike and lemony brightness to finish it off (we're being very picky here), so we usually ask for a side of the Dijon mustard. It does the trick, nicely balancing out the Maui onions. Meanwhile, the lemon risotto – we assume it's meant to provide the zesty lemon sparkle usually provided by the gremolata – is disappointing. The risotto tastes like it took a lemon bath before it reached your table. We leave it alone, or ask for the gnocchi.

That said, there is no doubt that the chef and his crew are deeply dedicated to their art and to the happiness and satisfaction of their diners. Every dish is infused with love, and we tend to agree with the waiter who suggested selecting by random pointing. It's possible to have a wonderful meal no matter what you eat.

Although the dessert menu reads deliciously, we're afraid that the pastry chef is not up to the standards of the head cooks. We'd skip dessert and order more appetizers up front, or splurge on a bottle from their excellent wine list. Capische? has been given the *Wine Spectator* Award of Excellence three years in a row (2004-6) for good reason, and your waiter can help you pick something perfect if you feel stuck.

The servers are dressed in black from head to toe, and they are all knowledgeable about the menu and the preparations. We notice that (unlike most restaurants on Maui) when we ask for something, we get it nearly immediately, rather than when they get around to it. It's sad that our standards are low enough to praise this level of attention, but hey, that's Maui. Uniformly professional and friendly, we always feel genuinely welcome and secure in the staff's hands.

The location really can't be beat. The Diamond Hawaii Resort is one of our favorite places (see Restaurant Taiko review for more detail), and Capische?, which rents out this space, has taken the original walled Japanese rock garden and transformed it into a lush, intimate, Italian herb garden which is harvested for dinner each night. If your party has four or more, ask for the best table in the back corner of the garden, completely set apart and partially hidden by lush greenery, featuring unobstructed views of Wailea all the way down to the ocean and the islands beyond. The views from the upper lanai are also unimpeachable. The flagstone floors are roughly friendly underfoot, the linens a sophisticated mix of black and cream, and the setting terribly romantic. There is a piano in the small be-couched bar area, and the pianist is often joined by a soft-and-sultry vocalist or a cool cucumber of an upright bass player.

This is not the most Hawaiian of restaurants and it can't claim to be the only restaurant of its kind, like Mama's rightfully can. You could get great food like this elsewhere on the mainland or in Europe. But you can't get this view, this place, or this seamless experience of paradise anywhere else. This is one of Maui's best kept secrets - even many locals have never come here - and in our opinion, the best restaurant on island.

Hours: Daily 6pm-9:30pm ***Meals:*** Dinner ***Cost:*** $29-$48
Known For: Italian with French influence. ***View:*** Gorgeous views from high up on Haleakala overlooking Molokini, Kaho'olawe, and Lana'i.
Kid-friendly: Yes, no separate menu.
Alcohol: Yes, with a beautiful wine list.
Website: www.capische.com ***Reservations:*** Required
Credit Cards: All Major

Location: South Maui, Wailea Diamond Hawaii Resort, 555 Kaukahi St.
808-879-2224 ***How to Find:*** From Wailea Alanui Drive, turn left on Kaukahi St., just past the Kea Lani Resort. Follow to the end, where you'll find Diamond Hawaii Resort & Spa Hawaii.
Parking: Valet, limited parking in lot immediately to right as you arrive.

Top Place to Dance
CASANOVA

Ambience: 17 ***Food:*** 16
Service: 18 ***Value:*** 18
Overall: 69

Two of our dearest friends were married last year after meeting on a Casanova's Ladies Night Wednesday, when the Makawao joint checks its makeup and slips on a stunning little dress.

Wednesday Night Ladies Night is an important part of the Maui scene. But so is every other night at Casanova, where you can hear live music from local musicians (and not-so-local) like Willie Nelson, Taj Mahal, and Dave Mason, among many others. Check out their listings when you get here; it's worth a trip upcountry.

The drinks are potent and capable of inspiring great Casanova-like activities – at least until the hangover the next morning.

There's also great food. The wood-burning pizza oven produces authentic Italian pizza (a different species from the deep dish at BJ's in Lahaina), and for many it's the best pizza on the island, although we think newcomer Flatbread down the hill in Pa'ia has them beat.

Try the excellent osso bucco. And the unusual porcini mushroom-coated lamb chops are fascinating – they come with both a fennel mustard sauce and a red wine and onion reduction. The Fra Diavolo, hot, spicy, tasty seafood and tomato sauce over spaghetti, is also a favorite.

The main ingredient in Italian cuisine is love, and the Italian owners maintain a deep devotion to your palette. The focaccia bread is always a hit, they make their own mozzarella, and you should try the tiramisu, too.

The cavernous and art-filled restaurant has several different seating sections. The main dining room features a back wall of plate glass with a beautifully lit stand of bamboo beyond. This is a lovely way of making a nice view in a restaurant that doesn't otherwise have one. The effect is very romantic.

We won't guarantee that you'll meet the love of your life at Casanova's, but if you've already met, you might want to dine here one evening and do some stargazing later.

Hours: Daily, Lunch 11:30am-2pm, Dinner 5:30pm-9pm
Meals: Lunch, Dinner ***Cost:*** $15-$45 ***Known For:*** Italian, Pizza
Kid-Friendly: Yes ***View:*** None, but interior is beautiful and romantic. Bamboo scene in the back of restaurant. ***Alcohol:*** Yes, full bar.
Website: www.casanovamaui.com ***Reservations:*** Recommended
Credit Cards: All Major

Location: Upcountry, Makawao 1188 Makawao Ave. ***808-572-0220***
Parking: Street or lot on the side of building.

Top Onion Rings

CASCADES GRILLE & SUSHI BAR

Ambience: 23 ***Food:*** 21
Service: 21 ***Value:*** 21
Overall: 86

Hotel restaurants are notorious for being overpriced and less than stellar. Who can really blame them? With a steady flow of customers who don't want to drive for a better meal, it's all too easy to justify cutting some slack.

Cascades Grille & Sushi Bar at the Hyatt Regency defies this stereotype . . . except when it doesn't. If you go on a great night, you'll be seated quickly, get good and efficient service, and dine on delicious food while looking at a marvelous view. On not-so-great nights one or all of these might suffer. We haven't personally experienced this, but we've heard enough stories to make a caveat up front.

The cuisine is fairly straightforward: steak and seafood in the open dining area with a stellar view of the ocean, and sushi in the enclosed sushi bar. Both menus are available no matter where you sit in the restaurant.

Please order the onion rings. One inch thick slices of sweet Maui onions are flash fried in a crunchy batter that crinkles on your tongue. They come in a bamboo basket and are served with two dipping sauces, a barbecue and a Thai chili pepper sauce that is sweet, spicy, and tangy all at once. Heaven.

The steaks really shine here. The cuts of Angus beef are very good, and the local Kula lavender and sea salt rub they use adds an unusual but lovely flowery note. We also like their simple pinot noir reduction and the meaty Hamakua mushrooms.

The fish is good, although we haven't yet found a preparation we think is good enough to top Pacifc'O's or Plantation House's concoctions. We do, however, heartily recommend the Seafood Mixed Grill. Lobster tail, scallops, prawns, and fish are piled high atop a bed of jasmine rice with a papaya beurre blanc sauce. The grill gets it exactly right – all are cooked to perfection, tender, and divine. The portion is generous and the price - $38 at last trip – cannot be beat.

We also like the Bento Box, a good way to get an outrageous quantity of food for less than $40. The "box" arrives in the form of a giant rectangular plate divided into six sections, each of which contains one of the following: a petite filet mignon, mahi mahi with coconut curry sauce, a green salad loaded with vegetables and dressed with caramelized pineapple sauce, jasmine rice, a California roll, and miso soup.

The sushi is not as good as elsewhere – we'd go to Sansei over ordering here. We'd also ask for an outside seat, since sitting inside the sushi bar tends to be hotter even with the air conditioning running due to the doors constantly opening and closing.

The restaurant is perched above the beach walk in Ka'anapali, so you are close to the beach but not stared at by passersby. The waterfalls and pools are gorgeous, and this is a very romantic setting. We think, for a hotel restaurant, this is well above average.

Hours: Sushi 5-10pm, Dinner 5:45-10pm ***Meals:*** Dinner
Cost: $40 and up ***Known For:*** Sushi, Seafood, Steak
Kid-Friendly: Yes, kid's menu ***View:*** Pacific Ocean and Hyatt pools.
Alcohol: Yes, full bar. ***Website:*** www.maui.hyatt.com
Reservations: Recommended ***Credit Cards:*** All Major

Location: West Maui, Lahaina 200 Nohea Kai Dr. in the Hyatt Regency
808-667-4727 ***How to Find:*** Drive all the way down the road until you are in the turnabout in front of the Hyatt Regency ***Parking:*** Valet

---

CHARLEY'S RESTAURANT AND SALOON

Ambience: 13 ***Food:*** 14
Service: 16 ***Value:*** 15
Overall: 58

We wish we could like Charley's better than we do. Its relaxed wagon wheel ambience, expansive menu, friendly service, and reasonable prices are enough to take us most of the way to happy. The fact that Willie Nelson plays on a regular basis should take us over the top, but we just can't ignore the fact that whenever we stop in for anything other than breakfast, we want to delegate the meal-eating to someone else.

Plenty of defensive locals who've made Charley's their favorite meeting place will disagree with us. They'll say the food is "fine" and the pizzas are "good." We think they're indulging at the bar in the back of the restaurant while making those judgments. The food is not fine - with the exception of breakfast, which we'll cover - and the pizza, despite the claim of "Maui's best" on the menu, is no better than Pizza Hut. We've had mixed vegetables crumpled from over-microwaving, stale croutons on salad dressed with food service dressing, and meatloaf that is cold in the center but piping hot and even burnt on the outer edges.

This is no better than cafeteria food, and when you're listening to a concert at night and throwing back a few microbrews, that might be OK, especially at these prices. But if you want to pay attention to and enjoy your food, we suggest eating elsewhere and then having a drink here during the show.

This is a local favorite, as evidenced by the blown-up photos of local windsurfers and the giant replica of Willie Nelson's guitar. But it's none too clean, and while a roadhouse dive can be appealing, it feels downtrodden, not charming.

Breakfast at Charley's is a better deal. The portions are huge, the kitchen seems to make more meals from scratch, and the coffee comes quickly. Locals flock here, so arrive early if you're on the way to Hana. Don't overlook other Pa'ia eateries for the same meal, though - we especially like Moana Bakery up Baldwin Avenue.

Hours: Daily 7am - 10pm ***Meals:*** Breakfast, Lunch, Dinner
Cost: $15-30 ***Known For:*** Breakfast, Pizza, Sandwiches
Kid-Friendly: Yes ***View:*** None, but a ceiling high replica of Willie Nelson's guitar (including autographs) is prominently displayed on the way to the restrooms.
Alcohol: Yes, full bar ***Credit Cards:*** All Major

Location: Northshore, Pa'ia 142 Hana Hwy ***808-579-9453***
How to Find: On the Hana side of the intersection with Baldwin Ave., right next to Jacque's ***Parking:*** Lot next to or behind restaurant, street.

CHEESEBURGER IN PARADISE/ CHEESEBURGER ISLAND STYLE

Ambience: 19 *Food:* 18
Service: 17 *Value:* 21
Overall: 75

We have mixed feelings about the Cheeseburgers (by the way, this is not Jimmy Buffet's mainland chain). Although the food is good and the drinks are very good, there's something a little forced about these restaurants. Their party hearty mien doesn't ring quite true.

Maybe, despite what the excellent menu copy promises, it's not such a party to work there. Every waiter– including the guys - wears a tiny grass hula skirt over their shorts or skirts. And the management-mandated "sassy attitude" doesn't always feel like a performance.

Meanwhile, the lava flows are excellent, as are the mai tais. A basket of seasoned fries and lightly breaded, thickly sliced onion rings is a must-order.

Our favorite burgers are the Royal Ali'i (fried egg and bacon), the Black and Blue (blue cheese and bacon), and the Guacamole (fresh guacamole made here, very good with chunky tomato and light on the garlic). All burgers are more than big enough to satisfy any appetite.

Other items on the classic American menu include coconut shrimp, potstickers, tuna salad sandwiches, excellent thick-sliced BLT's, chicken sandwiches, turkey burgers, and lots of salads for those who like veggies over meat.

The Lahaina location has stunning views of the harbor and open-air dining, as well as up to ninety minute waits (no reservations taken at either location). The music is loud and sometimes live, and the place is crowded and noisy. Kids love this restaurant. The restaurant in the Shops at Wailea is more sedate. It used to have an ocean view, but condos have been built that obstruct it. It's still open-air, though, and a good choice if you're at the mall and don't want to do the more upscale Longhi's. We've even seen weddings celebrated here.

The prices are rock-bottom for Maui – you'll spend about $10, sometimes less, on a burger – and as long as you can resist the clever menu marketing for their incessant line of logo products, your wallet should be happy. The t-shirts ***are*** pretty cute, though, and make good souvenirs, as do the tiki mugs and cheeseburger earrings.

If you're in the mood for a loud American burger joint, this is definitely your place.

Hours: Breakfast, 8am-11am; Lunch/Dinner: 11am-10pm
Meals: Breakfast, Lunch, Dinner ***Cost:*** $9-13
Known For: Breakfast, Burgers, Sandwiches ***Kid-Friendly:*** Yes
Alcohol: Yes, full bar ***Website:*** www.cheeseburgerland.com
Credit Cards: All Major

Location: West Maui, Lahaina 811 Front St. ***808-661-4855***
How to Find: It anchors the seawall on the right-hand side facing the ocean
Parking: Large parking complex by Hard Rock Cafe
View: Right on the ocean, unbelievable views.

Location: South Maui, Wailea 3750 Wailea Alanui Drive ***808-874-8990***
How to Find: In the Shops at Wailea ***Parking:*** mall parking lot

---

Top French
CHEZ PAUL RESTAURANT

Ambience: 20 *Food:* 24
Service: 23 *Value:* 20
Overall: 87

Even thinking about foie gras, crispy duck, and port wine reductions makes our mouths water and our eyes well with tears. French haute cuisine elevates mere ingredients to high art, and the very best chefs are slaves to the palette and the knife as much as any painter is.

Maui is blessed to have Chef Patrick Callarec, owner of Chez Paul, a tiny French oasis in the middle of a scrubby section of nowhere. You might be tempted to just blast by on your way in and out of Lahaina, but don't. We are tempted to stop every time we drive into Lahaina for yet another so-so meal at outrageous prices, so please take advantage of your freedom to eat only wonderful food, if only for our sakes.

Look for the low-slung, rather ramshackle building next to a local fruit stand. The large, bright red-white-and-blue sign above the door and the tiny gourmet market will signal you've found the place. (The market is stocked by the chef/owner, so if you love the foie gras make sure you come back and buy some the following day for a decadent beach picnic or a nourishing meal on the road to Hana.)

Inside, you'll find a few dozen tables, cozy couples, and groups of friends. Locals, celebrities, and visitors in the know all bask in the warmth of the waitresses' smiles and slim glasses of sauterne. A brick wall dominates the décor with lacy curtains, blue floral wallpaper, and matching upholstery softening the look. Candles, white tablecloths, fresh roses, mirrors, and prints create a romantic atmosphere where you can really focus on your companion(s).

The wait staff is uniformly friendly, terribly knowledgeable, and sweetly, genuinely attentive . . . to the point of opening the door for you on the way in and holding it open for you as they wish you ***bonne nuit***.

There is a full bar, and a nice-but-limited wine list. Unfortunately, most of their wines sold by the glass are from California. A bottle of yellow label Veuve Cliquot sells for $110, which is a fair price for Maui. (Note: If you want to celebrate with Veuve some night in your hotel room, get it at Costco for around $42 or at Long's for about $50.)

Most bread served on Maui is by necessity soft and doughy with nearly no crust (for a good thick crust you need air laden with bacteria and smog). The bread here is worth noting. The waitresses put your loaf in the oven right after they seat you, so that ten minutes later you have a warm, nearly toasted loaf that makes the crust much more satisfying than most here on island.

The complimentary amuses-bouche of Vichyssoise is creamy and perfectly chilled (not cold), with pine nuts and chives floating on the top. The bowl is ample and heralds good things to come, especially in the appetizer category.

We love the foie gras. Try the classic terrine with fruit chutney, Hawaiian sea salt, mango, and edible flowers ($28). Served with a hearty slab of toasted brioche, this is the part of the meal we like to linger over. Also on the plate is a thinly sliced pear that's been soaked in honey and white wine for two days. Absolutely divine. If the chef is in the mood to make it, the seared foie gras with fruit is also a delicious choice.

When the sea scallop appetizer with red pepper coulis and pineapple chutney is available, it's another excellent option. The scallops are perfectly seared, and their slightly sweet ocean flavor plays nicely with the sweeter pineapple and the much spunkier coulis.

The appetizers are so good that they set the bar very high for the entrees. Not that they're bad . . . they just don't transport us quite as much as the first courses do. Our very favorites include the rack of lamb, crispy duck, and the fish of the day poached in a champagne and cream sauce. They also serve a delicious lobster, if the season is right and your wallet can bear it.

The rack of lamb is delicious, but not formidably presented. A beautiful cut of meat is marinated in a dark, rich paniolo sauce and surrounded by a sweet and chunky chutney made of exotic fruits. We counted mango, pineapple, and perhaps apples in our last meal.

The crispy duck is Tahitian in origin. They serve the breast meat sliced and laid gently atop a thick and juicy leg. The skin is very crispy, the meat exceedingly tender, and overall very well-prepared. The island twist comes, once more, in the exotic fruit chutney that perfectly balances the salty crispness of the duck.

The portions are not huge, but they are worth every penny. The good news is you will probably still have room for dessert. They feature a beautiful hot and runny chocolate cake, seasonal berries in cream, and of course, a cheese plate.

In our "job" we are forced to eat many crème brulees. While that may sound like a perk, it isn't. Apparently, this simple custard-with-caramelized-sugar crust is beyond most pastry chefs. Chez Paul's pineapple and vanilla crème brulee served in a pineapple shell and garnished with lychees, strawberries, and other fresh fruits is a refreshing twist on a perfectly executed standard.

If for some reason you do not make a dinner reservation at Chez Paul, consider attending their lunch from 11:30am to 5:30pm. The menu is limited mainly to appetizers, but we think those are their forte anyway. You can also get the cheese plate, and there is always an entrée and dessert special. You won't get a price break, but you can sample the best French on the island at your convenience. ***Bon appétit!***

Hours: Daily, 5:30pm til close, 8:30pm is last seating ***Meals:*** Dinner
Cost: $32-$55 ***Known For:*** French ***Kid-Friendly:*** Yes, no separate menu
View: Stunning. None, but you will feel like you're in a little French hideaway
Alcohol: Yes, full bar ***Website:*** www.chezpaul.net
Reservations: Required ***Credit Cards:*** All Major

Location: West Maui, Olowalu Olowalu Village ***808-661-3843***
How to Find: On the Honoapiilani (Hwy 30) between Ma'alaea and Lahaina, mile marker 15 ***Parking:*** In front of restaurant

Top Mexican

CILANTRO FRESH MEXICAN GRILL

Ambience: 18 ***Food:*** 20
Service: 15 ***Value:*** 22
Overall: 75

Even though the name sounds like an upscale and modern place, Cilantro has some of the cheapest food on island. This fast-food Mexican restaurant prides itself upon serving delicious, fresh, healthy food, and you will not be disappointed if you check it out for a fast lunch or an inexpensive dinner.

The story goes like this: owner and chef Pris Nabavi wanted a fresh island take on "Old Mexico," so he went and studied with the living masters of the cuisine, the people in interior Mexico cooking everyday for their family and friends.

After collecting recipes and learning techniques that haven't changed in hundreds of years, he came back to Maui and incorporated our island foods into these ancient recipes. The result is simply wonderful.

The corn tortillas are hand-made in the exhibition kitchen by chefs wearing t-shirts that read "Si, I'm being fresh with you" on the back. Meanwhile the retired tortilla presses are painted in bright colors and hung in a place of honor on the gold-yellow walls with "Los Soldados Muertos" (retired soldiers) stenciled above.

Over the order counter is painted "Alohahola!" and over the door on your way out is "Alohadios!" Behind the counter you'll see giant jars of chiles and bins of bright produce. This place is just plain fun, with bright walls, bright art, and bright mirrors everywhere. And like the sign says, the food is infused with Aloha, which, when we use it here, means "divine love."

Good tortilla chips are essential, and Cilantro doesn't disappoint. With a salsa bar that features (at last count) five salsas, ranging from mild to crazy hot and including green tomatillos, you'll be happy with your munchies.

We love the simplicity of this food. Everything is fresh and bright on the plate. We haven't found anything with the life cooked out of it.

Try the roasted chicken anything. They rotisserie the chicken after letting it soak in herbs and citrus. The result is succulent chicken, still plump with its own juices, perfectly balanced and pleasantly astringent. We especially love the Mother Clucker Flautas. Take two flour tortillas, slather them with chicken and secret spices, roll them up and flash fry them, and then top with crema fresca and roasted jalapeno jelly. Sounds totally decadent, greasy, and belly-ache inducing? Nope. Light, crunchy, flavorful, and totally satisfying.

We also like the grilled fish. Flaky white opakapaka holds up well to the spicy, garlicky sides. The spicy jicama slaw is excellent. The jicama's crisp, rather sweet base notes are blended beautifully with chile and lemon (sometimes heavier on the lime). Lovely.

The salads are generous and hearty. Start with the mariposa salad with the tequila-lime vinaigrette; add pork, chicken, steak, fish, or shrimp, and you are a very happy diner.

Tacos, enchiladas, rellenos, tamales, burritos, chimichangas . . . you really can't go wrong. And while the ambience is decidedly noisy and not particularly intimate, you could make a fun little party of a meal if you take advantage of their BYOB policy. Dos Equis, anyone? Foodland is right next door.

Many locals eat lunch here several times a week. Feel free to do the same. And while you're in there, do us a favor and ask them to open a South Maui location.

Hours: Monday - Saturday 11am - 9pm; Sunday 11am - 9pm
Meals: Lunch, Dinner ***Cost:*** \$5-\$13 ***Known For:*** Mexican
Kid-Friendly: Yes ***Alcohol:*** Bring Your Own Bottle
Website: www.cilantrogrill.com ***Credit Cards:*** MC, VS

Location: West Maui, Lahaina 170 Papalaua Ave. ***808-667-5444***
How to Find: In the Old Lahaina Center next to Jamba Juice.
Parking: Parking Lot

CINNAMON ROLL FAIR

Ambience: 5 ***Food:*** 17
Service: 15 ***Value:*** 15
Overall: 52

Rainbow Plaza on South Kihei Road features a Denny's, Lappert's Ice Cream, and several little stores selling sarongs, slippahs, and Maui-inspired souvenirs.

Just underneath Denny's you'll also find Cinnamon Roll Fair, featuring a small counter stocked with sandwiches, muffins, and trays of delectable, sticky, gooey cinnamon rolls (our favorites on the island).

They have a choice of toppings they'll put in little plastic takeaway cups, including a creamy icing that we insist you try.

Hours: Monday-Friday 6am-7pm; Saturday-Sunday 6am-5pm
Cost: $4 ***Known For:*** Cinnamon Rolls, Breakfast
Kid-Friendly: Yes No Credit Cards

Location: South Maui, Kihei 2463 S. Kihei Rd. ***808-879-5177***
How to Find: underneath Denny's Restaurant ***Parking:*** mall parking lot.

Top Picnic Lunch To-Go

CJ'S DELI & DINER

Ambience: 17 *Food:* 19
Service: 16 *Value:* 20
Overall: 72

CJ's is a down home restaurant with an ambitious goal: homemade "comfort food" served by friendly people at reasonable (even inexpensive) prices. Can it be done in pricey West Maui? Apparently so.

The big, open restaurant is painted orange and gold with huge handwritten menus plastered against the back wall. Everything sparkles, even the kitchen behind the counter, and this is clearly a well-loved place. Tables are packed together and packed with people from open to close, and families love this place.

The food is good, but very good for the price. Nothing on the menu costs more than $15, and most cost under $10. You'll find great breakfast deals including sweet bread French toast and pancakes, but also sandwiches, fish plates, roasted turkey, and deli meats from New York for meals later in the day. Watching them grill actual corned beef for their classic Reuben makes the New Yorker in Molly go as melty as the Swiss cheese on top. Salads are good and made with fresh local ingredients.

We think the greatest deal going, however, is the Hana Box Lunch. For $12 you get a deli sandwich (roast beef, turkey, pastrami, corned beef, ham, egg salad, tuna salad, or chicken salad) with the lettuce, tomato, and toppings wrapped separately so nothing gets soggy on the journey. A bag of chips, a bottle of juice or soda, and their unbelievably delicious Road to Hana brownie are included. If you don't have a cooler already, they rent you one for a $5 deposit, and you can keep it the length of your stay on island. They'll even give you free refills on ice until you return it.

If you're on the west side, this should be one of your must-visits for home cooked comfort food with a break from resort prices. And if you're on the West side and driving to Hana, get your lunch here before you head out. You won't be sorry you did (see review for Tutu's).

Hours: Daily 7am-8pm ***Meals:*** Breakfast, Lunch, Dinner
Cost: $15 and under ***Known For:*** Breakfast, Boxed Lunch, Burgers, Sandwiches, Seafood ***Kid-Friendly:*** Yes, kid's menu
Alcohol: Bring Your Own Bottle ***Website:*** www.cjsmaui.com
Credit Cards: AX, MC, VS

Location: West Maui, Lahaina 2580 Keka'a Dr. ***808-667-0968***
How to Find: in the Ka'anapali Fairway Shops on the Honoapiilani Hwy. ***Parking:*** Shopping center.

COLLEEN'S AT THE CANNERY

Ambience: 18 ***Food:*** 20
Service: 17 ***Value:*** 19
Overall: 74

We walk into Colleen's and feel instantly comfortable. The high ceilings, black leather booth, antique sidebars, and open kitchen/counter area make it feel like an Irish pub, but the fresh white walls and ceiling fans signal Hawaii.

With early morning breakfasts that pack the joint to drinks at night, this place is jumping around the clock. Upcountry has a great deal going here.

The breakfast omelets are reasonable and tasty at $8.50, and the Eggs Benedict come in several different styles - from ham, bacon, lox, veggie, crab, mahi mahi, and ono - all ono (good).

The tofu vegetable wrap is a favorite, as is the prosciutto tapas plate. Add a latté (very good) and you're all set for the day.

At lunch, you can't go wrong with a big salad topped with the mahi mahi or ono. Or if you're really hungry, get the beef burger (Maui Cattle Company beef, hormone free) and add fries and a pint of beer, all for $10.95.

At night, the wild mushroom ravioli is good, as is the New York strip steak. The wine and beer list is short but decent. They make their own bread daily, and the espresso is excellent. This is a great alternative to Pa'ia if you want to be a little off the beaten path.

Hours: 6am to around 10pm nightly ***Meals:*** Breakfast, Lunch, Dinner
Cost: $10-$35 ***Known For:*** Breakfast, Coffee, Salads, Seafood, Steak
Kid-Friendly: Yes ***Alcohol:*** Yes, full bar. ***Website:*** www.colleensinhaiku.com
No Reservations Taken ***Credit Cards:*** AX, MC, VS

Location: Upcountry, Haiku 810 Haiku Rd. ***808-575-9211***
How to Find: Turn onto Haiku Rd. from the Hana Hwy, in the Haiku Marketplace right in the town center. ***Parking:*** In front of restaurant

---

Top Bistro Grill
Top Pie
DAVID PAUL'S LAHAINA GRILL

Ambience: 22 *Food:* 21
Service: 23 *Value:* 21
Overall: 87

While we don't agree with the many locals that think this is the best restaurant on Maui (Capische? is our favorite), we do like it very much. Perhaps it's the gorgeous setting with high-polish floors, pressed-tin ceilings, elegantly draped tables, and a central bar that tempts you to forgo your table and belly up. Perhaps it's the walls aglow with big, bright oil paintings that make this into almost a garden setting. Maybe it's the excellent service - the best on Maui - and the sophisticated bustling bistro ambience that harkens back to our city-living days.

While the food doesn't always live up to the ambience and the service, it reliably ranges somewhere from Very, Very Good to Excellent. And - lucky stars! - the pastry is even better. David Paul's has one of the few good pastry chefs on the island in their on-site bakery, and the rolls you begin your meal with will prove it. The butter that accompanies them is blended with thyme, rosemary, garlic, salt, and pepper, and loads up your palette with delight.

Standouts in the appetizer menu include steamed Manila clams in a white wine and parsley broth served with herbed garlic crostini (there's that bread again) and a kalua duck quesadilla bursting with roasted Maui onions and spiked with poblano peppers. The chef is not afraid of bold flavors or spices, and usually wields them with discrete and strategic precision.

We also like the plate of three separate seafood appetizers called the Cake Walk. The first "cake" is a Kona lobster crabcake with scallops, crab and a panko binding. While we feel strongly that there is too much binding, we like the mustard sauce that accompanies the dish. The sweet Louisiana rock shrimp cake also suffers from way too much cake and far too little shrimp. However, the seared ahi cake is delightful. A darling cut of ahi is laid over a patty of rice with the lightest, simplest, cleanest wasabi sauce we've had on the island.

Other starters include several very good salads, including a wonderful bufala mozzarella tomato salad with truffle oil and balsamic splashed over thickly sliced, perfectly ripe, intensely flavored tomatoes from Hana. This is one of our favorite dishes due to its simplicity and focus on excellent ingredients. The Caesar salad is also very good. A quarter of baby romaine lettuce is draped with anchovies, shaved parmesan, and dressed in a deliciously light garlic anchovy dressing.

For entrees, we like the Kona coffee lamb, with a reservation. The sauce of Kona coffee and a cabernet demi-glace is delicious and rivals Pineapple Grill's version for flavor . . . but we wish it were less a sauce and more a marinade. The meat - while perfectly prepared - cries for a longer immersion in the sinfully good sauce. That said, the carefully frenched rack makes the best presentation on the island, and the mashed potatoes that accompany it are perfect.

The osso bucco is very good, tender and served with gorgeous glazed root vegetables that melt in your mouth. The duck however, is a disappointment. We like the smoky flavor, but the dry texture is less refined than mealy. Vegetables served on the side are usually perfectly done, for example the asparagus crunchy and sprinkled with sea salt.

The cuts of fish are always perfect and perfectly cooked, but we're going to be picky because this is such a good restaurant. The ahi, which is a popular dish, is perfectly executed against a Maui onion and sesame seed crust - but only after scraping the crust off! Maui onions are exceptionally sweet, and we feel strongly that nearly every dish featuring them needs something more sharp to balance out that sweetness. The apple-cider-and-soy-butter vinaigrette used in this preparation is not nearly punchy enough to pull the fish out of the cloying onions, and when you pile it on top of vanilla bean rice, you've got dessert in the form of fish. The mahi mahi fares better with its delicious beurre blanc sauce, but the pancetta addition doesn't deliver what the imagination promises.

We love the tequila shrimp and firecracker rice, however. The spices are perfectly balanced - order this only if you like spicy foods - and the shrimp is pillowy and tender under the smooth-but-tangy tequila butter. This dish is a winner.

Their lovely dessert menu is really worth saving room for. As we mentioned, the pastry chef is doing wonderful work, and he should be rewarded. The Road to Hana, Maui is one of our favorites. Chocolate cake, chocolate mousse, and a delicious macadamia nut caramel are layered and topped with an S-curved crisp. The crème brulee is also good, but our favorite is the triple berry pie. Raspberries, blueberries, and black currants in a thickly satisfying crust topped with whipped cream . . . we actually buy this pie to freeze at home.

The excellent wine list (heavy on California), amazing service and the top-notch food combined with an upscale ambience makes this restaurant a contender for our favorite every time we visit. While there may be too much bustle for a truly intimate dinner, the romance quotient is high for those who don't mind urban settings.

Hours: Daily 6-10pm ***Meals:*** Dinner ***Cost:*** $40 and up
Known For: Steak, Seafood ***Kid-Friendly:*** Yes, kid's menu
Alcohol: Yes, full bar ***Website:*** www.lahainagrill.com
Reservations: Recommended ***Credit Cards:*** All Major

Location: West Maui, Lahaina 127 Lahainaluna Rd. ***808-667-5117***
How to Find: Just off Front St. near Cheeseburger in Paradise.
Parking: Street, behind the restaurant (pay)

DOWN TO EARTH

Ambience: 15 ***Food:*** 16
Service: 12 ***Value:*** 17
Overall: 60

With the fast food chains packing Dairy Road, you might miss this healthy alternative, and that would be a shame. This chain health food store is not the best whole food store on the island (Mana Foods in Pa'ia is), but it's the most central and it has the best takeout/prepared food counter. It's also overwhelmingly vegan and all organic.

Self-serve stations feature hot and cold items, including salads, lasagna, chili, curries, millet cakes, mock tofu chicken, curried tofu (great, with apples, cashews, and raisins), and Greek salad. You pay by the pound, and can take out or eat in with the locals at the stools and tables available in the upper loft.

While you're there you can pick up vitamin supplements, bulk groceries, produce, or energy bars.

Hours: Monday-Saturday 7am-9pm; Sunday 8am-8pm
Meals: Breakfast, Lunch, Dinner ***Cost:*** $7-$15
Known For: Healthy, Organic, Prepared Foods, Salad Bar
Kid-Friendly: Yes ***Website:*** www.downtoearth.org
Credit Cards: All Major

Location: Central Maui, Kahului 305 Dairy Rd. ***808-877-2661***
How to Find: Across from the Maui Marketplace
Parking: In front of store.

Top Chinese

DRAGON DRAGON CHINESE RESTAURANT

Ambience: 17 *Food:* 19
Service: 19 *Value:* 21
Overall: 76

This is the only good Chinese restaurant on Maui, and while we can't say that it's great, it is very good. If you're craving Chinese, it will do the trick.

Be prepared for glacial temperatures – on an island that sets air conditioning at a warmish 80 degrees, the 70 degree temps inside this restaurant will feel like actual weather.

Meanwhile, the service is excellent, and the prices are fair. Family style dishes are good, and the few dim sum dishes at lunch are well worth the $3 price tag.

Any special made with fresh local Hawaiian fish is likely to be a standout. Sometimes they have a steamed whole fish with a tasty black bean sauce. If you're with a large group, they have a number of large tables with Lazy Susans in the middle, so everyone can try all the foods you order. The Dungeness crab is delicious. The meat pulled from the claw is sweet and tender.

During the holidays this restaurant has fixed price specials for groups of six or more people, but make sure you call for reservations ahead of time.

There's good feng shui with a pretty fish tank, and beautiful Chinese art on the walls. You'll find Dragon Dragon just down the walkway from the best movie theater on the island with stadium seating. We often find ourselves here pre- or post-film.

After you're finished, forgo the desserts and head down the mall to the world-famous Tasaka Guri-Guri ice cream shop next to the pet store (see review).

Hours: Daily 10:30am-2pm, Monday-Friday Dinner from 5pm-9pm
Meals: Lunch, Dinner ***Cost:*** $10-$25 ***Known For:*** Chinese
Kid-Friendly: Yes ***Alcohol:*** Yes, full bar
Reservations: Required for special meals like Christmas Day Dim Sum.
Credit Cards: All Major

Location: Central Maui, Kahului 70 E Kaahumanu Ave. ***808-893-1628***
How to Find: Maui Mall, next to IHOP ***Parking:*** Mall parking lot.

Top Kobe Beef

DUO

Ambience: 19 ***Food:*** 19
Service: 23 ***Value:*** 19
Overall: 80

Duo is one of those restaurants designed to leave you so full and so satisfied at breakfast that you won't mind coming back here for dinner. As the main dining establishment at The Four Seasons (Ferraro's Bar e Ristorante across the pool has been around longer, but is more casual and Spago, located upstairs from Duo, is not run by the resort) it has a big responsibility: fulfill every culinary wish and dazzle with friendly, down-to-earth, white glove service.

For the most part, Duo succeeds admirably. We love breakfast here. The buffet features everything from pastry to fish to miso soup to made-to-order omelets, and the poolside location with the Wailea beach beyond is a view that really can't be beat. If you're on Maui during a special holiday like

Mother's Day or Easter, check to see if they're having a champagne brunch – it promises to be decadent, satisfying, and perfectly executed.

Duo at dinner is a slightly different story. While the service is always top-notch, the ambience in the restaurant doesn't quite transform from upscale day-time poolside to luxury fine dining the way they intend it to. As for food, what can shine during the day loses its luster at night.

The restaurant's logo has a fish tail and a cow's head, indicating the "duo" surf and turf theme on the menu. Everything is listed separately: fish, meat, sauces, and sides. Nothing is paired for you – you can choose any cut of meat and pair it with any of the meat sauces. You can choose any fish, and pair it with any of the fish sauces. If you can't decide on one sauce, they will happily bring out two, or three, or all of them for you to try. The sides are served family style and are ordered separately from the entrees.

This is all very exciting at first. It feels liberating: At last! A chef who trusts me and lets me have exactly what I want! But, as one of our foodie friends who's spent a long time in the restaurant business pointed out during a recent dinner, "I may like the flexibility to choose what I think I would like, but I also want to know what the chef's opinion is. I get lost on this menu."

Part of the problem is pure formatting. Everything is listed on one single panel – by our count over fifty items – and in small type. It makes us feel like throwing up our hands and saying "One of everything, and bring all the sauces, too!"

Our favorite appetizer is the ahi sashimi, which is significant, since all the kitchen needs to do is correctly slice an excellent cut of fish in order to make sashimi work. The goat cheese fritters – made with the excellent local cheese from Surfing Goat Dairy – are less than stellar. The cheese is delicious, but the breading it's "frittered" in adds nothing more than a crunch, and the ratatouille that accompanies it is mostly a vegetal echo of the cheese's texture.

The stars on this menu are definitely from the "Land," and the brightest of the bunch is the fabulous Japanese Kobe beef. The cuts available vary by the day, and by the time you dine they may be sold out. This is the only place on Maui to offer you genuine Japanese Kobe, and it's sold by the ounce (minimum orders apply, at $27-$29 per ounce). If you've never splurged, do so, and savor every bite. The "regular" filet mignon is very good and comes in a 10oz. and 7oz. size, so most appetites can be accommodated. We are partial to this cut over the rib-eye, and definitely over the T-bone. Whatever you choose, it will be cooked perfectly.

The sauces available include béarnaise, peppercorn, merlot, barbecue, horseradish, shallot jus, and herb-garlic butter. They come in their own little serving dishes arrayed around your entrée, so that you may dip into each individually rather than have the kitchen dress your meat.

We vote for the merlot. It is the best balanced and the best reduction, but it still isn't as good as it should be . . . which begs the question "Who is the saucier?" When there are two sauce sections on your menu - one for meat, one for fish - you ***must*** have an outstanding chef dedicated to sauce. If every sauce shone, then it would be a joy to mix and match. As it is, it's more an exercise in "will this one be better?"

The available fish are usually ahi, opakapaka, mahi mahi, lobster, and prawns. All are prepared simply and presented on a plate with your choice of sauce in a little dish. The sauces include orange-butter, pineapple-papaya salsa, lemon-caper butter, Thai red coconut curry, Hawaiian teriyaki, and salsa verde. We like the pineapple papaya salsa the best.

There are several different potato sides to choose from, including fries that look amazing but taste oily and have a flabby texture. Luckily they come with little potato crisps that are fun and crunchy and make marvelous little treats. The homemade ketchup is too sweet, but the truffle oil aioli that comes with these is the best thing on the table. We ask for an extra little bowl and use it as a sauce for . . . everything.

We like the cream spinach over the sautéed version. The Kula corn "off the cob" is absolutely delicious, buttery, sweet and summery.

Duo has an excellent wine list, with all wines grouped according to their body and characteristics rather than their varietals. All big, loudmouthed reds are listed together while the dainty, fruity whites cluster farther along the menu, and so on. The effect is that even novices can read the wine list and get a pretty good idea of what they should order. This kind of attention to detail and description would be well served on the main menu.

A very fine restaurant gently instructs your mind while it entertains your palette. Sometimes the main lesson is "I didn't know food could taste this good." But we notice that at establishments where nothing is a standout, the waiters can telegraph that to you by not being able to tell you much beyond what the menu does. That's been our experience here at Duo. When pressed for opinions, the servers often resort to "It's really up to you and depends upon what you like." While this may be true - diners do have the right to order what they like - this could also be interpreted as an indirect way of saying "I can't wholeheartedly recommend anything, so please just choose something you'll be happy with."

Overall, we like Duo, especially for their breakfasts and brunches. The food at night is also good - but it doesn't match Spago just upstairs, Capische? up the hill, or even Longhi's at the Shops at Wailea. Duo has yet to celebrate its first anniversary, so that may change over time.

Hours: Daily 6-11:30am, 5:30-9pm ***Meals:*** Breakfast, Dinner
Cost: $40 and up ***Known For:*** Breakfast, Brunch, Buffet, Kobe Beef, Seafood, Steak ***Kid-Friendly:*** Yes, kid's menu
View: pool, beach, and the West Maui Mountains beyond.
Alcohol: Yes, full bar ***Website:*** www.fourseasons.com/maui/dining/duo.html
Reservations: Highly recommended, especially for champagne brunch.
Credit Cards: All Major

Location: South Maui, Wailea 3900 Wailea Alanui Dr. ***808-874-8000***
How to Find: Lower lobby, Four Seasons Resort
Parking: complimentary valet

FAT DADDY'S SMOKEHOUSE BBQ

Ambience: 18 ***Food:*** 17
Service: 17 ***Value:*** 19
Overall: 71

Texas barbecue is its own beast. The meat (usually beef) is slow-cooked with low heat and smoke over wood chips for anywhere from seven to twelve hours. Even when it's fully cooked, the meat remains pink due to the preserving action of the smoke. Meanwhile, there's a thick layer of char on the outside that carries the wood flavor with intensity. Sauce, which can be sweet or spicy, vinegary or tomato-based depending upon the chef, is served on the side or just dashed over the top, so the chef can prove their meat is high quality.

Fat Daddy's opened on July 4, 2007, in Kihei, and so far they're doing Texas right. The ribs are tender inside with a nice pink color, and the brisket is tender and tasty too. Their smoker is doing a good job imparting a hearty wood flavor, and they're not leaving the meat in too long and getting the bitter taste that can come with this method. Brats and pulled pork are the other two meats featured on the simple menu, and they both rate a solid "good."

Fat Daddy's barbecue sauce is super-sweet on its own - almost cloying. But when paired with the intense char of the meat itself, the combination gives a good, balanced taste.

They have all the traditional sides you'd expect - beans, cole slaw, macaroni and cheese, watercress salad, corn bread, rice, and corn. The beans are watery but flavorful, with a slight smoke to them that we like. They're not too sweet, and if you can forgive the soupy presentation and just focus on the beans, we think you'll like them. The mac 'n' cheese is exactly what you would expect at a homemade barbecue – lots of white cheese (probably Monterey and cheddar), lots of macaroni, and nothing surprising. The watercress salad has less cress than Napa cabbage and carrots . . . but it's a good salad with a "secret" dressing. (We think that secret is pretty obviously sesame oil.) The cornbread is stacked high and hearty, but we really want a nutty, home ground taste, not the smooth, oiled texture this bread offers.

Overall, we like Fat Daddy's. The prices are great for Maui – a "fat plate" is your choice of meat and two sides for $10 to $12. The colored walls, long bar area, and open floor plan make the small space look more capacious than it is, and the owner (who grew up in Texas) and staff are friendly and easygoing. If you like Texas barbecue – and some don't – we think you'll do OK here.

As one of the newest restaurants on island, we hope they stick around, and we look forward to freshening our reviews on a regular basis.

Hours: Daily 11:30am-3:30pm; Dinner 5-8pm ***Meals:*** Lunch, Dinner
Cost: $10-$16 ***Known For:*** Barbecue
Kid-Friendly: Yes ***Alcohol:*** Yes, full bar.
Credit Cards: All Major

Location: South Maui, Kihei 1913 F&G S. Kihei Rd. ***808-879-8711***
How to Find: In Kalama Village, across from Foodland, next to Life's a Beach.
Parking: Kalama village parking lot.

Top Lu'au Food

FEAST AT LELE

Ambience: 23 ***Food:*** 20
Service: 18 ***Value:*** 18
Overall: 79

Feast at Lele is run by the excellent chef James McDonald, who also runs two of our favorite restaurants, I'O and Pacific'O. Nestled on the beach behind the 505 Front Street center, this upscale lu'au features private tables, complete service, and fabulous views of the harbor.

The more intimate ambience and the five course meal served at table make this a much more romantic lu'au than the well-established and much awarded Old Lahaina Lu'au. But the entertainment suffers in comparison, and the food isn't always as good as it should be given the quality of ingredients (excellent) and the kitchen (superb).

Each of the courses features traditional food from a specific region of the South Pacific: Hawai'i, New Zealand, Tahiti, and Samoa. The entertainment features dances from each region also, so you learn as you go in a full-sensory experience.

While the food is traditional, it's updated with some Hawaiian Regional Cuisine twists. This is good for us food lovers, since traditional Hawaiian food is ***not*** fine cuisine. Two decades ago grilled fish and poi, macaroni salad, and greasy pig were de rigeur. Then the Hawaiian Regional Cuisine movement started, championed by chefs like Maui's own Bev Gannon, Roy Yamaguchi, and Mark Ellman, and cuisine in the islands vastly improved.

The drinks are excellent – and since they're all you can drink, we suggest you partake. Stay overnight in Lahaina if you're coming from South Maui, or take a cab back to your hotel to avoid the truly dangerous highway, so you can really party. The mai tais and lava flows are delicious (and strong) but we really like the Banana Madness with a hint of Irish cream liqueur. There are several beers and wines available, and if you want to pay extra a whole series of after dinner drinks are available.

If we graded the show as if this were elementary school, we'd give it a halfhearted B with a NI for Needs Improvement. There's a feeling that the performers are here because they couldn't hack it over at Old Lahaina, and while they usually have genuine smiles on their faces, their feet often look like they're just going through the motions. On the other hand, the fire dance at the end is always fun to watch, and several acts begin with a canoe pulling onto the beach.

When deciding upon a lu'au - and yes, we think you should do at least one - the choice really comes down to which you value more - the food, or the show?

Old Lahaina will give you a better overall experience, and the show is wonderful, but you sit at long tables with strangers and stand in a buffet line to get "authentic" food from steam tables.

The more private Feast at Lele will give you a more intimate meal with better service and more HRC-style food, but the show drags and can feel beside the point.

If you don't feel a burning need for the whole lu'au experience - which really is fun - but want to make a point of trying the cuisine, we recommend spending your money at Mama's, the most Hawaiian of all restaurants, and ordering the traditional lu'au meal.

Hours: Daily at sunset, 6pm-9pm ***Meals:*** Dinner
Cost: $105 plus tax for adults, $75 plus tax for children 12 and under
Known For: Hawaiian, Lu'au, Polynesian ***Kid-Friendly:*** Yes
View: Amazing, directly on the beach. ***Alcohol:*** Yes, full bar and all inclusive.
Website: www.feastatlele.com ***Reservations:*** Required.
Credit Cards: All Major

Location: West Maui, Lahaina 505 Front St. ***808-667-5353***
How to Find: At the very back of 505 Front St., past the shops, enter between I'O and Pacific'O.
Parking: Street, or lots across from or underneath 505 Front St.

FERRARO'S BAR E RISTORANTE

Ambience: 22 ***Food:*** 21
Service: 23 ***Value:*** 18
Overall: 84

Ferraro's is one of our favorite places for what we call a "civilized lunch." The setting – an open terrace shaded by giant tented umbrellas overlooking the ocean – is gorgeous, and the food is top notch. The service, of course, is Four Seasons sterling. Our favorites include the Maine lobster sandwich with avocado spread on toasted sourdough bread served with Kula baby greens, although Jim prefers the version they used to serve on focaccia bread (ask, they'll make it for you). We also like the quattro stagioni pizza – artichoke hearts, Portobello mushroom, prosciutto and Gaeta olives. Crispy crust from their wood-burning oven serves as the perfect base for their excellent quality toppings. Fresh salads are also tasty and heartily portioned.

At dinnertime, this location serves up a gorgeous sunset, but in our opinion the overall quality of preparation goes down along with the sun.

Our favorite dish is the fritto misto calamari and shrimp appetizer. The breading creates perfect crunchy clouds floating around the tender fish. The sauce is a spicy tomato and our only complaint is that we wish for more. Ask for a side bowl to supplement the usual serving.

The signature lobster risotto is delicious fish with disappointing risotto. The lobster tail is perfectly done – the best we've ever had. The generous tail is grilled and laid on top of a bed of lobster risotto that has the claw meat sautéed and mixed in to the rice. Tiny tricolor tomatoes are strewn throughout, and they provide juicy mouthfuls. But not even these darling touches can rescue this risotto. There is just way too much tooth to this rice, which should be milky and creamy from a long, luxurious, well-attended stirring.

Another popular and highly recommended dish that we have trouble with is the lamb with macadamia nut crust served with polenta and wine-poached pears. The sauce is little more than a reduction of the lamb juices, and while it is meaty and hearty, we want something with more complexity to stand up to those nutty, rich macadamia nuts. The polenta is also disappointing. Although it has a lovely crunchy parmesan crust on top of the small round cake, the polenta itself has little of the smooth corn flavor we're looking for. We just want . . . a little something more.

We like the veal pappardelle better. This hearty ragu served over wide noodles is filled with chunks - the menu calls them "cheeks" - of veal that has been braised until hearty, juicy, and bursting with flavor. This is good eats! The noodles are very good, but can get a tad oily from the ragu.

The Italy-centric wine list is excellent and comprehensive, but they can also bring a selection of California and French bottles over from their sister restaurant Duo. The selection by glass is weak with only one featured Chianti, but the bottle prices are fair considering you're at the Four Seasons.

The meal ends with a coffee press, our favorite way to serve. And one of our favorite desserts on the island is on this menu, the apple tart. Flaky pastry lays down for thin slices of apples, a delicious caramel sauce, and a generous crumble. Next to that a round cookie is layered with a scoop of macadamia nut ice cream, and a paper-thin slice of candied apple. Every single item on this plate is excellent on its own and even better paired with everything else.

While we love the location of this restaurant, we would choose it for lunch over dinner. For a really fine, romantic Italian meal at sunset we'd head up the hill to Capische?

Hours: Daily 11:30am-9pm ***Meals:*** Lunch, Pupus, Dinner
Cost: $27-52 ***Known For:*** Italian ***Kid-Friendly:*** Yes, kid's and teen menu
View: Terrace over the ocean, absolutely beautiful ***Alcohol:*** Yes, full bar.
Website: www.fourseasons.com/maui/dining/ferraro_s_bar_e_ristorante.html
Reservations: Recommended for dinner ***Credit Cards:*** All Major

Location: South Maui, Wailea 3900 Wailea Alanui Dr. ***808-874-8000***
How to Find: Between the pool and the beach at the Four Seasons Resort
Parking: Valet

FIVE PALMS RESTAURANT

Ambience: 21 ***Food:*** 18
Service: 17 ***Value:*** 20
Overall: 76

Five Palms has the best oceanfront location in Maui. Molokini twinkles in the near distance, and Keawakapu beach stretches out all the way to the Wailea resorts. It's stunning.

Outdoor seating is best, of course. But if you're inside (which you could be at busy dinner hours) the décor is kind of fun retro-1960's Hawaiian and the open shutters let in the breezes. The restaurant is in the Mana Kai Resort, a rather staid high-rise we don't recommend staying in.

The food here is fine, especially at breakfast and lunch. With both served daily from 8am to 2:30pm, you can get your burger in the morning (ick) or your crepes in the afternoon.

The garden benedict, with spinach and sun dried tomatoes, is very good. So is the outrageous banana foster pancakes, with bananas caramelized in a rum/pineapple juice libation.

The Five Palms probably has the best burger in Maui, made with Angus beef and grilled perfectly. The spinach salad with bacon, blue cheese, candied walnuts, and citrus vinaigrette is also a favorite. And the French dip is ***tres bien***.

For dinner, try the Szechuan rack of lamb or the prime rib. The fish is okay but not spectacular, and no matter how tempting the Hawaiian Bouillabaisse looks, don't order it. We recommend SeaWatch for fish.

Half-priced pupus from 3 to 6pm make this a GREAT early bird special and the romantic yet casual atmosphere makes this a great option for most couples on vacation, as well as families. Be prepared for slow and sometimes half-hearted service.

If you're here during Easter week, make reservations for their Easter champagne brunch buffet. It's spectacular, and you'll probably see us there with at least a dozen friends.

Hours: Daily, 8am-9:30pm, bar 'til 11pm ***Meals:*** Breakfast, Lunch, Dinner
Cost: Breakfast and Lunch: $7-15; Dinner: $25+
Known For: Breakfast, Seafood, Steak ***Kid-Friendly:*** Yes
View: Spectacular, one of the best on Maui. ***Alcohol:*** Yes, full bar
Website: www.fivepalmsrestaurant.com ***Reservations:*** Recommended.
Credit Cards: All Major

Location: South Maui, Kihei 2960 S. Kihei Rd. ***808-879-2607***
How to Find: Turn right after Kihei Boat Ramp.
Parking: In front of restaurant, valet on special occasions.

Top Pizza

FLATBREAD COMPANY

Ambience: 20 ***Food:*** 24
Service: 18 ***Value:*** 23
Overall: 85

"At Flatbread, the food is sacred. More often than not, the first bite of one of our flatbreads, for a first time customer, is very nearly a spiritual experience."

That's a quote we found on the Flatbread Company website. Sound a little over the top? It's not. This is the best pizza we've ever had in our lives. Hands down!

Pizza is very difficult to make on our beautiful island. At least, that's what pizza makers have been telling us for years. Flatbread Company, a New England chain that we are happy to welcome to the island, has the magic touch.

The fact that they use spring water, organic flour specially milled for them, kosher salt and cake yeast has something to do with the unbelievable crust on this pizza. The sauce is delicious, organic tomatoes and a dozen fresh/organic/natural herbs. Toppings are free-range, organic, or natural and all amazing. But in food this good, you know the real secret ingredient is L-O-V-E.

Our favorite pizzas are homemade sausage (nitrate-free maple-fennel sausage, caramelized onions, sun dried tomatoes, mushrooms, mozzarella and parmesan cheese, garlic oil and herbs, or get with the tomato sauce, it's just as good) and Pele pesto (basil, macadamia and garlic pesto with chevre goat cheese, roman tomatoes, kalamata olives and herbs). But they're all amazing. The toppings are so fresh that you can't go wrong. You can also make your own combinations.

Salads are wonderful (try the pineapple vinaigrette dressing), and try the Julia's Homemade Banana Bread dessert, too.

The lemonade sweetened with maple syrup is a taste of home for New Englanders - and done absolutely right here.

The service is genuine and heart-felt, if somewhat spotty when they're busy. The big main dining room offers lots of different seating options, including a bar, booths, tables, and couches with coffee tables. The outside lanai has both booths and big communal tables. The restaurant is noisy (all Pa'ia restaurants seem to be) but it doesn't matter when you're eating pizza this delicious. Bring the kids, they'll adore it.

Hours: Daily, 11:30am-10pm ***Meals:*** Lunch, Dinner ***Cost:*** $10-$20
Known For: Organic, Pizza, Salads ***Kid-Friendly:*** Yes ***Alcohol:*** Yes
Website: www.flatbreadcompany.com ***Reservations:*** Not required, but you might want to call ahead in the evenings. ***Credit Cards:*** All Major

Location: North Shore, Pa'ia 89 Hana Hwy ***808-579-8989***
How to Find: Across from Maui Hands just after you enter town from Kahului. ***Parking:*** Street

FRED'S MEXICAN CAFÉ

Ambience: 18 ***Food:*** 17
Service: 18 ***Value:*** 19
Overall: 72

When Fred's opened up in early 2006, locals were excited. We don't have much good Mexican on Maui, and sometimes you get a craving for fajitas and 'ritas that nothing else will satisfy.

Fred's didn't disappoint at first. The fresh ingredients, careful preparation, and outstanding flavors blew us away. The margaritas were great, and nothing on the menu was over $10.

Well, the prices have crept up a little, and the overall quality has gone down a bit in this San Diego import. But they still satisfy basic cravings for margaritas, especially for those of us unable to get to Pa'ia for Milagros' version.

The homemade chips and salsa arrive almost immediately, spiking your thirst for the 20 oz. house margarita at a very reasonable $6. Their tequila menu is wide-ranging and their upsell tactics are pretty good - your drink might just cost more than your meal. They've also got Dos Equis and several other beers on tap, which come in the same 20 oz. margarita glass.

Fajitas are usually very good (although at lunchtime the veggies tend to be greasy and soggy). We highly recommend the steak version, which comes in a perfect medium rare.

Tacos are also very good and only $2 on Tuesday nights. The shredded chicken version is our favorite, with the steak a tie. The mahi mahi tacos ***sound*** great, but head to Maui Tacos up the street for those. Fred's just aren't as good as they should be, and there's plenty else to eat here.

They also have burritos, enchiladas, nachos, and other standard Mexican preparations. And their burgers are surprisingly good with a nice flame-broiled char.

We would not recommend the pork, in any of the dishes. It's marinated but not slow-cooked, so the meat is flavorful only as you suck the marinade off. After that it's just white mush.

The appetizer they call Chingaderas are very popular, but we don't care for them. We have nothing against fried foods, but these fried burrito pieces dipped in egg batter and breadcrumbs are just plain yucky.

This is a good restaurant for families, even though the bar scene is big in back. It's a noisy, crowded place with good food and great prices. The service is usually very good for Maui. With a great location right across from Kamaole Beach II and breezy seating, we'd say it's a good bet if you're looking for a casual restaurant and a good drink.

Hours: Daily, 7am-11pm ***Meals:*** Breakfast, Lunch, Dinner
Cost: $10-$20, $2 tacos on Tuesday nights ***Known For:*** Mexican
Kid-Friendly: Yes ***View:*** Pretty if you're focusing on the ocean, not so pretty if there is a lot of traffic on S. Kihei Rd.
Alcohol: Yes, full bar and about 50 tequilas.
Reservations: Recommended, the wait can be up to one hour if you walk-in.
Credit Cards: All Major

Location: South Maui, Kihei 2511 S. Kihei Rd. ***808-891-8600***
How to Find: Across from Kamaole Beach II.
Parking: Street, limited in lot next to restaurant.

Top West Side Breakfast
GAZEBO

Ambience: 18 *Food:* 19
Service: 19 *Value:* 19
Overall: 75

This is a breakfast-and-lunch-only restaurant next to a pool in a condo complex in Napili (just north of Ka'anapali). Think you can just show up and find a seat?

No way. Think about when you want to eat, and then arrive about 30 minutes early (depending upon how crowded the island is) so you can get a table when you want it. No reservations.

There aren't many places we'd recommend waiting in line for, but . . . the Gazebo is a little different. A gorgeous ocean view will distract you while you wait. They have a free coffeebar available so you can caffeinate while you wait for a table.

We usually go for breakfast, where you can find Eggs Benedict, local fried rice plates, breakfast burritos, and great pancakes. Get bananas, pineapples, macadamia nuts, and white chocolate chips on your pancakes for a real paradisiacal decadent meal.

The omelets are also very good. All the usual fixings are featured, including avocado and wonderful shrimp. There are sandwiches, burgers, and salads if you're there at lunchtime. Overall, this is the place to be for west side breakfast, although if you don't want to wait you could go to Sea House just down the road or our favorite, Plantation House in Kapalua.

Hours: Daily, 7:30am-2pm *Meals:* Breakfast, Lunch *Cost:* $7-$15
Known For: Breakfast, Burgers, Sandwiches *Kid-Friendly:* Yes
View: One of the best on Maui. Lots of whales in season.
Reservations Not Taken - arrive early *Credit Cards:* MC, VS

Location: West Maui, Napili 5315 Lower Honoapiilani Rd. ***808-669-5621***
How to Find: Next to the pool in the Napili Shores Condo Complex.
Parking: Limited in Condo parking lot.

GERARD'S RESTAURANT

Ambience: 20 ***Food:*** 21
Service: 22 ***Value:*** 20
Overall: 83

Gerard's has been recognized by *Mobil Travel Guide*, *Bon Appetit*, and *Wine Spectator,* and we consider ourselves lucky to have this French gem here on island.

Gerard's is nestled in front of the Lahaina boutique bed and breakfast, The Plantation Inn. White tablecloths, candles, and white-gloved waiters with towels over their arms all telegraph high French cuisine and make up for the fact that there is no beach view. Gerard has been on Maui for a long time (since 1973), but he has never lost touch with his rigorous culinary training and his ancestrally-inspired passion for food.

All the best of French food is here, and most everything has a Hawaiian touch. You can get foie gras served with wine jelly - a classic dish with a twist of pineapple confit. You can also get foie gras served seared in a spice crust with poha berries - eat that, Paris!

Try the spinach salad, the cucumber soup, and the fresh ahi tartare with taro chips. The rack of lamb is to die for. A generous portion of thick and juicy meat is perfectly plated with potatoes au gratin sliced so thin they melt in your mouth.

Other excellent choices include the roasted Hawaiian snapper in an emulsion of orange, ginger, and fennel fondue, and the caramelized pork tenderloin with honey, rhubarb, and banana compote served with coconut curry sauce. The Hawaiian touches are always directly in line with the superb French food, and only enhance, never detract.

Gerard makes his own sorbets and they are light and refreshing. The whole dessert menu is tempting, so save room.

The wine list is lovely, and you are sure to find just the right pairing for your meal. The service is friendly, genuine, and attentive, and the waiters clearly love working here.

If you are an Inn guest, you get a luscious breakfast at Gerard's. Locals have been jealous of that ever since Gerard's stopped making their amazing weekend brunches.

Although the fairy-lit garden several blocks from the ocean may seem second-rate when compared to other restaurants' beach views, we don't miss it once the food starts arriving. We highly recommend Gerard's for special meals on the west side.

Hours: Daily, 6-8:30pm ***Meals:*** Dinner ***Cost:*** $30-40
Known For: French ***Kid-Friendly:*** Yes ***View:*** Pretty garden or well-appointed interior ***Alcohol:*** Yes. ***Website:*** www.gerardsmaui.com
Reservations: Recommended ***Credit Cards:*** All Major

Location: West Maui, Lahaina 174 Lahainaluna Rd., Lahaina
808-661-8939; 800-661-8939
How to Find: On the first floor of the Plantation Inn.
Parking: Limited in parking lot, also on street.

Top Tiramisu
GIAN DON'S ITALIAN BISTRO

Ambience: 20 *Food:* 20
Service: 19 *Value:* 19
Overall: 78

Gian Don's serves good food at reasonable prices in a pretty, relaxed restaurant with live entertainment most nights of the week.

The homemade pastas are some of our very favorite items. The vodka rigatoni is nicely balanced - not too creamy, tomatoey, or spicy. The ravioli are pillowy, tasty, and comforting.

The fish dishes are very good. Opakapaka served in the Italian preparation is our favorite. Garlic, onions, and tomatoes sizzle in a little olive oil with some light herbs, perfectly complementing the delicate taste of the pink snapper. Mahi mahi and salmon are also available most nights, and while you may be tempted by the Island preparation of pineapple salsa and champagne dressing, we recommend you stay with the heartier Gian Don preparation: crab, mushrooms, and tomatoes in a zingy lemon butter draped with mozzarella cheese. This works particularly well on the mahi mahi or the salmon.

We are surprised at how much we like the ribs here, and even our friend from Kansas City says they're great, and "better than any Italian restaurant on Maui has a right to serve." The tropical-flavored plum barbecue sauce is smooth-sweet-tangy, and the rib meat is tender and juicy. The $11 appetizer version is a generous enough portion for a light dinner. Salads are very good and fresh, and we think the $7 blue cheese salad with bacon, onions and tomatoes is one of the best deals on the island.

Gian Don's wins our vote for best tiramisu on Maui!

The polished tile floors and the high ceilings make the dining room rather noisy, especially when the live entertainment gets going in the evenings, but the service is attentive and knowledgeable.

We occasionally eat breakfast here as an alternative to Big Wave or Kihei Café. Since it sits a little higher above South Kihei Road, not directly next to it or on a parking lot, the al fresco dining feels a little more luxurious. The prices for breakfast are on par, and the food is almost as good as those two places.

Hours: Daily 7:30am-9:30pm ***Meals:*** Breakfast, Lunch, Dinner
Cost: $13-30 ***Known For:*** Italian ***Kid-Friendly:*** Yes.
Alcohol: Yes, full bar. ***Website:*** www.giandons.com
Credit Cards: All Major

Location: South Maui, Kihei 1445 S. Kihei Rd. ***808-874-4041***
How to Find: next to Maui Dive Shop ***Parking:*** lot behind the restaurant

---

Top Sunday Brunch

GRAND WAILEA GRAND DINING ROOM SUNDAY BRUNCH

Ambience: 24 ***Food:*** 20
Service: 17 ***Value:*** 19
Overall: 80

There is nothing small or half-way about Grand Wailea Resorts (see our Bistro Molokini or Humuhumunukunukuapua'a review for fuller resort descriptions). If you're looking for a fantastic champagne Sunday brunch in Wailea, you can't go wrong making reservations here.

You get to the Grand Dining Room by walking through the open-air lobby and down the sweeping staircase. The dining room is designed and decorated as a paradisiacal version of Versailles - soaring arches, celestially painted ceilings, heroic statues and giant wall frescoes with Hawaiian history themes. Comfortable chairs and heavy tables dressed in white linens complete the island elegant look.

As for the view of the resort and the Pacific, the only word we have to describe it is "sweeping."

Normally we would warn you about slow service at the Grand restaurants, but for brunch you only rely on the staff for coffee and champagne, so it's not as much of a problem. You can stay as long as you like, returning over and over to the six food stations to indulge.

The champagne is very good, and you can get it in a tart-sweet fresh-squeezed mimosa if you feel like it. The food is very good, but not excellent (there's only so much you can do to keep buffet food fresh. . .it always suffers from sitting around in warmers). There are a few notable exceptions to this, however.

The omelet station features a range of fresh ingredients and a competent chef to assemble them on your plate. The carving station features the usual suspects, including a very succulent prime rib and racy horseradish cream. Also, if they have it, try the ham baked in bread dough, which leaves the pink meat juicy from the inside layers out.

We also like the homemade malasadas. You can watch the pastry chef deep fry these crispy-on-the-outside-doughy-in-the-middle Portuguese treats right at the station. They serve the traditional cinnamon-sugar version, but also a decadent cream filled malasada.

You'll also find plenty of fresh salads, rice, fish, chicken, and the usual shrimp, sushi rolls, and cheeses. Soft Maui bread is mounded on every station, and you can find waffles and eggs benedict in the trays. The bacon is thick and hearty, and the dessert table filled with beautiful sweets. Nothing stands out as being wonderful - again, the pastry chef problem on Maui - except for, when they have them, the chocolate covered strawberries. These are really delicious, and a simple-yet-sinful way to end a decadent meal.

This is an excellent Sunday champagne brunch and a beautiful way to while away a Maui morning.

Hours: 10:30am-1pm ***Meals:*** Brunch ***Cost:*** $50
Known For: Breakfast, Brunch, Buffet ***Kid-Friendly:*** Yes
View: Gorgeous of the Grand Wailea Resort and the ocean.
Alcohol: Yes, champagne, full bar ***Reservations:*** Recommended.
Website: www.grandwailea.com ***Credit Cards:*** All Major

Location: South Maui, Wailea 3850 Wailea Alanui Dr. ***800-888-6100***
How to Find: In the Grand Wailea dining room down from the twin spiral staircases. ***Parking:*** Valet

---

HAKONE

Ambience: 21 ***Food:*** 21
Service: 21 ***Value:*** 19
Overall: 82

The Maui Prince Hotel has one of the best sushi restaurants on the island in Hakone. Spacious and elegant, but casual and intimate, this is one of our favorite places to "get away from Maui" and celebrate a special occasion.

The food is impeccably done. The sushi is fresh, the presentation gorgeous, and the service from kimono-clad waitresses is attentive and unobtrusive. The sake list is extensive, and you'll find several tasting options available if you're interested in trying something new.

We've never eaten anything we didn't love. Some favorites include the light-as-air tempura, the cucumber salad with snow crab and seaweed in a snappy vinaigrette, and the miso butterfish. The baked lobster in a creamy white miso sauce is absolutely divine - simple flavors come together to form a much better than expected rich taste.

Their coursed dinners are a decent value, like the $60 Rakuen Kaiseki, seven courses starting with appetizers and ending with dessert. You can even make your entrée the lobster tail.

If you make reservations on a Saturday evening, you're in for one of the best deals on the island, the Japanese Buffet. For under $50 (and half that for kids) you can eat all you want from salads, sushi, seafood, entrees, and desserts. Try the marinated salmon sashimi, steamed clams, snow crab legs, prime rib, pork and cabbage, baby back ribs, spicy tuna rolls, pumpkin and cranberry salad . . . and so much more that it makes our eyes well just thinking about it.

Hours: Tuesday-Saturday 6-9pm ***Meals:*** Dinner ***Cost:*** $40 and up
Known For: Japanese, Sushi ***Kid-Friendly:*** Yes
View: Ocean view through plate glass windows.
Alcohol: Yes, full bar plus excellent sake list.
Website: www.princeresortshawaii.com/maui
Reservations: Recommended ***Credit Cards:*** All Major

Location: South Maui, Makena 5400 Makena Alanui Dr. ***808-875-5888***
How to Find: In the Maui Prince Hotel
Parking: Free parking to the left as you enter, or valet

Top Upcountry Restaurant

HALI'IMAILE GENERAL STORE

Ambience: 19 ***Food:*** 22
Service: 20 ***Value:*** 20
Overall: 81

Hali'imaile (Hah lee ee my leh) General Store is Maui's celebrity restaurant. The slogan is "It's all about food and Bev!"

Bev Gannon is one of those mega-star chefs (cover shots on *Food & Wine*, list of *Gourmet's* "best tables," etc.) who has never gone to a formal culinary school. She opened Hali'imaile in 1988, and Maui has never been the same since. Her cuisine is solid, well-made comfort food. It's what our dinner-party-loving grandmothers would have made forty years ago had they known what to do with fish.

Hali'imaile General Store is a refurbished location in the pineapple "district" on the way up Haleakala. Because it's far from the beaten path, locals love it and tourists tend to miss it.

The interior is decorated with colorful pottery and big bright paintings. The hardwood floors and bright, open space make for a welcoming, homey atmosphere. Seats in the back of the restaurant tend to be a little more private, but we like the party scene at the front tables. Just be prepared for the lack of air conditioning during the hotter summer months, because it can get toasty, especially at lunch (this is reflected in our ambience ranking).

The drinks are great. Make sure you try the lilikoi daiquiri or the mango-tini. And if you're not of drinking age, the Baby Blue Whale has your name on it (lemonade and blue oranges).

For appetizers, the signature dishes are crab pizza and sashimi Napoleon. We love the Napoleon - layers of sashimi, smoked salmon, caviar, and won tons on a bed of salad greens with a wasabi vinaigrette - and think it is a must order. It's so much fun to smash the won tons with a heavy steak knife and then scoop up all the layers at once and let the flavors play in your mouth. We skip the crab pizza with its much speculated "mystery ingredients."

The Chinese chicken salad is a favorite, as is the macadamia nut fish preparation. The rack of lamb is amazing either way you ask for it (comes in either a Hunan or mint preparation). The servers are very knowledgeable, so ask them for their opinions.

Kids don't go hungry here. No hot dogs on the menu, but there are pizzas, ribs, quesadillas, and barbecued chicken.

For dessert, everyone swears by the pineapple upside-down cake and the lilikoi brulee, but personally, we think the chocolate macadamia nut pie is the dessert to beat. It's a chocolate tart crust with a macadamia nut-studded chocolate filling - and Bev took it off the menu in 2005. When we ask why, all we get is some line about how it's "a winter dessert." If you want to make Jim *very* happy, ask them to put it back on the menu.

Hours: Monday-Friday, 11am - 9:30pm; Saturday & Sunday, 5:30pm-9:30pm
Meals: Lunch, Dinner, "Mini Menu" between 2:30pm-5:30pm
Cost: \$20-\$45 ***Known For:*** Hawaiian Regional Cuisine
Kid-Friendly: Yes, separate menu ***View:*** Sugar Cane fields.
Alcohol: Yes. ***Website:*** www.bevgannonrestaurants.com
Reservations: Recommended, especially for dinner.
Credit Cards: All Major

Location: Central Maui, Hali'imaile 900 Hali'imaile Rd. ***808-572-2666***
How to Find: Turn onto Hali'imaile Rd. from Haleakala Highway.
The restaurant is just past the pineapple cannery. ***Parking:*** Parking lot.

Top Smoothie

HAWAIIAN MOONS NATURAL FOODS

Ambience: 15 ***Food:*** 16
Service: 18 ***Value:*** 20
Overall: 69

Hawaiian Moons in South Kihei is the place to shop for health food if you don't want to drive to Pa'ia and go to Mana Foods.

This is a small, clean, well-stocked store with an excellent selection of groceries, produce, and vitamins and beauty items. While Mana and Down to Earth can carry everything, you can count on the folks at Hawaiian Moons to carry the best. Prices are a little higher than at those other stores, but OK for Maui.

Their takeout is exceptional. The salad bar is great, and many locals pick up their meals here. You can count on the food being fresh. The hot entrees are vegetarian and yummy. The smoothies are fresh, healthy, and the perfect break for when you're hot from Kamaole Beach I, across the road.

Hours: Daily, 8am-9pm ***Meals:*** Lunch, Dinner ***Cost:*** $8-$12
Known For: Healthy, Organic, Prepared Foods, Salad Bar
Kid-Friendly: Yes ***Credit Cards:*** All Major

Location: South Maui, Kihei 2411 S. Kihei Rd. ***808-875-4356***
How to Find: Same plaza as Quiznos and Maui Tacos ***Parking:*** Parking lot.

HULA COOKIES & ICE CREAM

This little ice cream store in Ma'alaea Harbor features the excellent Maui ice cream brand Roselani. They also make pretty good cookies, and a trip here will satisfy most dessert cravings.

Roselani is served in most restaurants on Maui, and you can buy it in just about any supermarket on the island. But we like it best here, scooped into a sugar cone. Try the Kona Coffee, which is literally the best coffee ice cream we've ever had (even better than Haagen-Dazs' super premium). The flavor is intense and unadorned. We also love the macadamia nut ice cream in either vanilla or chocolate. The simpler the flavor the better we like it, but some of our friends feel a tugging emptiness in their gut when a week goes by without a scoop of the chunky, fudge beribboned Kona Mud Pie.

For cookies, we like the coffee chocolate chip - a chocolate chip cookie with coffee added to the dough - for its simple twist on a familiar favorite. Try their ice cream sandwiches for a fun treat, two cookies with your choice of ice cream filling.

Hours: Monday-Saturday 10am-6pm; Sunday 10am-5pm
Meals: Ice Cream ***Cost:*** $4 ***Known For:*** Ice Cream
Kid-Friendly: Yes ***Website:*** www.hulacookies.com
Credit Cards: AX, MC, VS

Location: Central Maui, Wailuku 300 Ma'alaea Rd., Suite 207 ***808-243-2271***
How to Find: Near the Maui Ocean Center and across from the Pacific Whale Foundation ***Parking:*** parking lot

HULA GRILL

Ambience: 20 ***Food:*** 18
Service: 17 ***Value:*** 18
Overall: 73

We love the Hula Grill, but we like to sit outside in the Barefoot Bar rather than inside in the dining room. Once you're seated, kick off your slippers (what flip-flops are called on the islands, pronounced "slippahs"), and start playing in the sand. All the tables are oceanfront, thatched roof umbrella-ed, and the bar is one giant sandbox.

Order a Plantation Lemonade (citrus vodka, lemonade, and a splash of cranberry juice) or a mai tai (both happy hour specials), and sit back and relax, because it doesn't get more Hawaiian-themed than this on Maui.

The crab wontons are good pupus, and the salads are all top notch. You can make a nice meal out of pupus and salads, or you can order the fish, pizza, or the excellent burger with blue cheese.

In the dining room, the fare is more expensive, but just as good. The mahi mahi is nice, and try the ahi poke rolls - rare ahi wrapped in rice paper.

This restaurant is always busy, and the Whaler's Village location is parking-friendly and close to shopping.

The kid's menu is stocked with pizza, chicken, burgers - and free pasta for kids under four. With this and Hawaiian music daily, Hula Grill has done a lot of things right.

Hours: Dining Room, 5-9:30pm, Barefoot Bar, 11am-11pm
Meals: Lunch, Dinner ***Cost:*** $12-$35
Known For: Burgers, Sandwiches, Seafood, Steak
Kid-Friendly: Yes, separate menu.
View: Very pretty ocean view, Lanai in the background.
Alcohol: Yes, full bar ***Website:*** www.hulagrill.com
Reservations: Recommended ***Credit Cards:*** All Major

Location: West Maui, Ka'anapali 2435 Ka'anapali Parkway ***808-667-6636***
How to Find: Whaler's Village Shopping Center ***Parking:*** Parking lot.

HUMUHUMUNUKUNUKUAPUA'A

Ambience: 23 ***Food:*** 21
Service: 18 ***Value:*** 18
Overall: 80

Don't worry about trying to say the restaurant's name. Just call it "Humu's." Named after the state fish that swims in the lagoon that surrounds this restaurant, the word means "fish with a nose like a pig."

Like everything at the Grand Wailea, this restaurant is designed to look like paradise. It floats on a lagoon stocked with humus and other friendly fish, has a thatched roof, and the staff dresses in very old-school muu-muu's. It's very good theater, and the food rises to meet it.

The very best fish preparation is the sesame-crusted mahi mahi with veggies and a delicious black-bean miso sauce. The spiny lobster (you pick your own from the cage) is wonderful when grilled, and another favorite is the sweet corn and lobster soup.

Although the food is good, we have a big reservation about this restaurant: the service is notoriously slow. We choose Spago at the Four Seasons or Mama's Fish House in Pa'ia for as good or better food at comparable prices, with better service.

Hours: Nightly 5:30pm-9:00pm ***Meals:*** Dinner ***Cost:*** $32-$72
Known For: Hawaiian, Seafood ***Kid-Friendly:*** Yes
View: Gorgeous grounds and ocean - part of what you're paying for.

Alcohol: Yes ***Website:*** www.grandwailea.com
Reservations: Recommended ***Credit Cards:*** All Major
Location: South Maui, Wailea 3850 Wailea Alanui Drive
808-875-1234 ext. 4900
How to Find: Grand Wailea Resort, near the water bar ***Parking:*** Valet

---

Top Lahaina Restaurant

I'O

Ambience: 20 ***Food:*** 23
Service: 22 ***Value:*** 22
Overall: 87

We are unabashedly in love with James McDonald's upscale-but-relaxed I'O. The restaurant design is post-modern, the service is knowledgeable and friendly, and the food unquestionably at the top of the Hawaiian Regional Cuisine pyramid.

The appetizers are so strong here that we like to order a bunch and share . . . and they will course them for you if you adopt our strategy. Our hands-down favorite is the Thai curry asparagus soup. The creamy, smooth-as-silk liquid is outrageously flavorful and a beautiful creamy green color. A thin ribbon of spicy red pepper/tomato coulis spirals ever tighter into the center of the bowl, ending in the middle with a generous chunk of lobster.

Also try the crab cake with panko crust and a miso aioli on the side. We especially like the green papaya cole slaw that serves as a bedding for the crab cake. The grilled calamari appetizer is another must-try. A marinated steak of calamari (not rings and tentacles) is grilled just until tender, topped with a roasted tomato dressing and served with tabouleh. No crunchy crust on this calamari, and while it may surprise at first, the tender, delicately flavored white meat is really a star in this preparation. The portion is large enough to serve as an entrée.

We also adore the Mad Hatter, an excellent puff pastry filled with scallops, mushrooms, and chilies. This dish is somehow both light and hearty at the same time, and we reserve some of the excellent house bread just to sop up the lobster coconut curry. Otherwise we would have to resort to licking the plate.

For main courses, we recommend the crispy ahi in a seaweed and panko crust. The radish sprout aioli that accompanies sounds crazy, but tastes rich and earthy. If you really want to treat yourself well, go for the I'O Trio, a three-entrée combo including a small filet mignon, osso bucco, and seared fresh fish of the day with lobster curry, bedded by a mushroom risotto.

If you're more in the tasting mood, try their daily *crudo* ("raw" in Spanish) specials. Small dishes of fresh and marinated fish and seafood are often some of the best on the menu. Pair this with one of their scarily strong martinis, and you've got a really nice little starter.

They don't do traditional tropical drinks here (go across the way to their sister restaurant Pacific'O for excellent mai tais and lava flows) but focus on martinis and their wonderful wine list. *Wine Spectator* has awarded the list as "Excellent" and we agree – especially with so many reasonably priced wines by the glass. Each item on the menu has a wine suggestion underneath it, so you get lots of advice as you go along. You'll also find the waiters are knowledgeable and helpful when choosing.

From the glass aquarium sculptures at the entrance to the lanai seating outside, this restaurant feels like an upscale foodie oasis . . . and it is. The view is drop dead of Lahaina Harbor, and sitting on the rail rather than outside gives you a better view. It also insulates you from the music of Feast at Lele next door (this lu'au is a James McDonald production and actually shares I'O's kitchen). We like hearing the show, but if you prefer a less-noisy ambience make your reservations for later in the evening as things are winding down.

If you're choosing between I'O and her sister Pacific'O, the choice is basically in experience – Hawaiiana, or upscale? The food is excellent at both restaurants, although one I'O waiter bragged to us that when they hold their "Iron Chef" competitions up at the chef's gardens in Kula, I'O cooks always win. We suggest you might try both establishments during your visit.

Hours: Daily 5:30-10pm ***Meals:*** Dinner ***Cost:*** $28-38
Known For: Pacific Rim, Seafood ***Kid-Friendly:*** Yes, no separate menu.
View: Stunning, one of the best on the island.
Alcohol: Yes, full bar with great martinis ***Website:*** www.iomaui.com
Reservations: Recommended ***Credit Cards:*** All Major

Location: West Maui, Lahaina ***Address:*** 505 Front St. #114 ***808-661-8422***
How to Find: At the back of 505 Front St. shopping area.
Parking: In the lot across the street or underneath 505 Front St., street.

JACQUES BISTRO

Ambience: 17 ***Food:*** 19
Service: 17 ***Value:*** 20
Overall: 73

Eating at Jacques is like dining in an international open-air bazaar. Situated on a giant lanai under a sprawling tent with a sushi bar attached, you will hear at least three different languages at any given moment. The décor tends toward surfer dude, and the clientele are a scantily clad collection of beautiful people from all over the world who know how to ride the ocean swells. This is where they come to have a nice meal at the end of a long day.

Jacques attempts to serve all customers – whether islanders, Europeans, Americans, or Asians – a little something from home in every dish. This leads to a combination of flavors and preparation techniques that often surprise, and usually succeed nicely.

We especially like the pumpkin fish entrée. A pile of fish of the day layered with bananas and orange slices, then draped with a ginger pumpkin sauce and laced with miso butter . . . it sounds absolutely wild, and it is. The sweet of the fruit bounces off the dark ginger flavor and then rebounds off the miso, and the butter brings it all together. It is really unusual.

We also like the vegetable tofu curry dish, again featuring bananas and oranges in a coconut curry. Creamy, light, and playful. Absolutely delicious. If they have it on the menu, the duckling with the lilikoi (citrus), pumpkin, cumin, and cinnamon is both succulent and daringly sweet-spicy.

We also like their salads, the pumpkin coconut soup with diced scallops, and the steamed clams. The sushi bar makes a great spicy tuna roll.

The service is very good, although it can be distracting to be served by women who look and move like they belong on a catwalk. The mai tais at the bar are very good. The prices are fair for the quality and service, because Pa'ia customers tend to be sophisticated in palette but poor in wallet. Overall we recommend Jacques if you're in the mood for an upscale meal in an eclectic, international, fairy-lit circus tent.

Hours: Daily 11:30am-3pm, 5-10pm (Sushi bar closed Sunday. & Monday)
Meals: Lunch, Dinner ***Cost:*** $20 and up ***Known For:*** Seafood, Steak, Sushi
Kid-Friendly: Yes, no separate menu ***Alcohol:*** Yes ***Credit Cards:*** All Major

Location: Northshore, Pa'ia 120 Hana Hwy ***808-579-8844***
How to Find: Near the Minute Stop Gas Station ***Parking:*** Street

, 2008

SIMPLY DELICIOUS FOOD

Ambience: 20 ***Food:*** 20
Service: 20 ***Value:*** 20
Overall: 80

Bev Gannon has a penchant for out of the way locations. Her Hali'imaile General Store is in the middle of a sugar cane field, and Joe's is in the private Wailea Tennis Center. As you turn in, don't expect to see the restaurant immediately, as it's rather hidden. Just find a spot in one of the several small parking lots and wait for a golf cart to come by and pick you up.

The open-air restaurant has gorgeous views of the ocean and Lana'i to complement a truly spectacular interior. The 43-foot copper bar is comfortable and expansive, while the wide-planked floors, high rafters, and fresh breezes make you feel like you're eating on someone's home deck. This restaurant feels remarkably private and cozy despite the open floor plan. You can, however, hear the thwacking of tennis balls as they hit the court below.

The food is, as promised, simply delicious. (Warning: portions are L-A-R-G-E at Joe's. You may want to share. There is a hefty split charge of $10, but we think it's worth it.) The food is all comfortable American. You won't find any terrific surprises, but you won't find anything that doesn't taste great, either.

A favorite is the tender prime rib with garlic whipped potatoes, island veggies, and au jus. The Pan Seared Scallops are prepared perfectly, and the rich creamy shallot butter sauce highlights their tender sweetness. The ribs are also good, with grilled corn and steak fries.

The crab dip served with tortillas is our favorite appetizer, but the salad to order is definitely the Portobello with warm bacon vinaigrette over greens with blue cheese and sweet cherry tomatoes.

The service is very good, and the staff knowledgeable. We'd easily choose Joe's over most restaurants in the nearby Shops at Wailea for food, service, and views.

Hours: Nightly 5:30pm-19:30pm ***Meals:*** Dinner ***Cost:*** $26-$35
Known For: Seafood, Steak ***Kid-Friendly:*** Yes
View: Tennis courts, and the ocean beyond ***Alcohol:*** Yes, full bar
Website: www.bevgannonrestaurants.com
Reservations: Recommended ***Credit Cards:*** All Major

Location: South Maui, Wailea 131 Wailea Ike Place ***808-875-7767***
How to Find: Turn into the Wailea Tennis Center from Wailea Ike.
Parking: Park in any lot and wait for the golf cart to come pick you up.

Top Prepared Foods

JOHN PAUL'S FINE FOODS

Ambience: 18 ***Food:*** 18
Service: 18 ***Value:*** 18
Overall: 72

Oh, John Paul, how we love you. You have finally brought a truly upscale, homemade, hoity-toity-but-easy-going prepared foods store to Maui. And you put it in Pukalani, the surprisingly convenient but pleasantly hidden away little town between Makawao and Kula.

This small storefront in the Pukalani Square sells to-die-for comfort foods in their to-go case. Look for their incredible chicken masala, mac 'n' cheese (get the cheese sauce, too, sold separately), lasagnas, meat loaf, salads, and tomato soup. On the gourmet side you can't beat their honey/soy flank steak, caprese salad, and cous cous. The smoked shrimp are outrageous, and their chocolate chip cookies are crispy and chewy at the same time.

The menu changes based on local availability and the chef's attention, but they give samples of everything, so try before you buy.

They also sell sandwiches, dried fruits, crazy-high-end mustards and vinegars, local produce, and fresh flowers. And if you've never had the UK soda called Fentiman's, you should get a bottle or two. It's an artisanal soda made over several days and in several steps, and it's quite unusual. We especially like the Seville Orange Jigger.

Mana Foods in Pa'ia is easier to get to, but John Paul is careful to stock things no one else has, and only of the highest quality. This is an excellent place to do some gourmet provisioning if you're staying in a condo or rental and plan to cook while you're on-island, or if you're picnicking and want a meal to pack out.

Hours: Monday-Friday 10am-7pm, Saturday 11am-5pm
Meals: Prepared Food, Sandwiches ***Cost:*** $10 and under
Known For: Market ***Kid-Friendly:*** Yes.
Website: www.johnpaulfinefoods.com ***Credit Cards:*** All Major

Location: Upcountry, Makawao 81 Makawao Ave. ***808-572-7100***
How to Find: in Pukalani Square ***Parking:*** Parking lot

JOY'S PLACE

Ambience: 13 *Food:* 20
Service: 18 *Value:* 19
Overall: 70

Ask a vegetarian local in nearly-suburban Kihei where to grab a good lunch, and they'll invariably light up while they recommend Joy's.

Ask a carnivorous local in nearly-suburban Kihei where to grab a good lunch, and they'll invariably light up while they recommend Joy's.

Joy's wins our hearts for super-fresh, handpicked, consciously prepared lunches. And while there are plenty of hummus, avocado, sprouts, collard greens, and nut burgers on the menu, there is also outrageously delicious home-roasted free-range turkey and locally caught tuna.

Try the falafel burger, a homemade garbanzo bean patty on sprouted grain bread with homemade tahini caper sauce and clover sprouts. Too sprouty? Try the turkey avocado cheese sandwich. It's the best turkey sandwich we've ever had outside of our own post-Thanksgiving kitchen: succulent roasted turkey piled so high with provolone, avocado, lettuce and tomato that you can barely fit the entire concoction in your mouth. We also love the turkey salad: that same turkey mixed with a little mayo and celery, topped with well-balanced cranberry sauce.

Besides tempeh wraps, veggie burgers, fish-less sushi rolls, organic salads, and tuna salad sandwiches, there are also specials everyday of the week but Sundays when they close. If your kid is worried he'll hate the sprouts, you can get him a provolone, cheddar, or Swiss cheese sandwich . . . or peanut butter and jelly. They have sprouted grain bread and less-intensely healthy local herb bread.

Smoothies with spirulina and organic lemonades keep you hydrated and refreshed, but the main "joy" at Joy's is the care and attention they put into their work. These people are really dedicated to health and wholesome food, and they don't preach or preen - they just cook with love.

The one drawback is the price. All those great ingredients (they cut no corners here) means they charge what they need to. When you pay $10 for a sandwich - no matter how big it is - on a paper plate sans chips or drink, you know you're not at Subway. We often find ourselves balking at the prices, but we always forget the cost when the first mouthful hits our taste buds. Joy's is definitely worth a stop-in for lunch, and no one could be disappointed with the taste.

Hours: Monday-Saturday 10am-3pm ***Meals:*** Lunch ***Cost:*** $10
Known For: Healthy, Organic, Salads, Sandwiches, Smoothies, Sushi
Kid-Friendly: Yes ***Credit Cards:*** AX, MC, VS

Location: South Maui, Kihei 1993 S. Kihei Rd. ***808-879-9258***
How to Find: In the Island Surf Building on S. Kihei Rd. across from Kalama Park. Turn onto Auhana Rd. to park directly in front of the restaurant ***Parking:*** Street

---

Top Banana Bread

JULIA'S BEST BANANA BREAD

If you or your traveling partner has nerves of steel, you should drive around the West Maui Mountains from Kapalua to Wailuku. The views are unbeatable, the land wild and rugged, and the trade winds blowing in from the west make the air on this side crystal clear.

At times you may feel like you are taking your life in your hands as you make hairpin turns on roads that barely manage to cling to their cliffside perches. But it's worth it for the banana bread.

After a particularly gut-wrenching stretch you will find yourself in darling Kahakuloa (Kah hah koo loh ah), a little town on a little harbor with a little white church and a little pink shave ice stand and a little green banana bread stand.

Both stands deserve a stop, but we want to call your attention to Julia's Best Banana Bread. The bread is moist, succulent, and sweet, and you should buy a loaf. If you take advantage of her free samples, you *will* buy a loaf.

If you don't want to drive out to Kahakuloa, you can try her bread at Flatbread in Pa'ia. This is our favorite pizza place on island, and they source their desserts locally. The bread suffers from the ride over, and even dressed up in macadamia nut ice cream we don't like it nearly as well as we do in the original location, but it will do in a pinch.

Hours: bread is usually sold out by 2pm ***Cost:*** $5 for a loaf
Known For: Banana Bread ***Kid-Friendly:*** Yes
View: Unbelievable Credit Cards Not Taken

Location: North Maui, Kahakuloa
How to Find: On the Honoapiilani Hwy way past Kapalua ***Parking:*** small lot

---

KIHEI CAFFE

Ambience: 14 ***Food:*** 17
Service: 18 ***Value:*** 21
Overall: 71

Locals and tourists alike flock to Kihei Caffe for breakfast. The counter inside is manned by locals with true Aloha spirit, and the service is fast. This is a solid, good value in no-frills breakfast and lunch.

The coffee is good, as is the fresh OJ. The biscuits come with most egg dishes, and while they're not great, they're better than most attempts on

Maui. The pancakes are fluffy, and a stack of three will fill you up nicely. So will the mammoth cinnamon rolls. They're built for sharing, and we recommend you ask for the to-go box even if you're going to eat it there, just in case you want to save some for later (there will be enough).

The burgers are good and hearty, and so are the sandwiches. Ask for everything exactly how you like it – they'll be happy to oblige. This is one of those places where the owner and staff really seem to like serving you, and they do well because of it.

Hours: Daily, 5am-1:30pm for breakfast, 1:30pm-8pm for lunch
Meals: Breakfast, Lunch ***Cost:*** $6-$10
Known For: Breakfast, Burgers, Cinnamon Rolls, Sandwiches
Kid-Friendly: Yes ***Website:*** www.kiheicaffe.com
No Credit Cards

Location: South Maui, Kihei 1945 S. Kihei Rd. ***808-879-2230***
How to Find: In the Kalama Village Shopping Center across from the giant whale. ***Parking:*** Parking lot, street

---

KOBE JAPANESE STEAK HOUSE & SUSHI BAR

Ambience: 17 ***Food:*** 20
Service: 17 ***Value:*** 21
Overall: 75

Teppanyaki is a kid's dream meal. You sit with your family at a u-shaped table around a big hibachi grill while funny/serious men in white (or black or maroon) hats chop, sizzle, and sling dinner onto your plate. You get teased, you get extra fried rice because you're little . . . it's pure food theater. Or maybe we mean food circus?

In either case kids love it and we have to admit, we do too. Kobe is the island's only teppanyaki restaurant, and we're glad it's here. They serve good food, put on a fun show, and you leave feeling satisfied and nurtured.

That is, if you sit downstairs, where the air conditioning is strong enough to battle the heat from the grills and the ceilings are high enough to funnel extra smoke away from your lungs. If you sit upstairs it's a different experience altogether. Even with the air cranked all the way, it is barely adequate for comfortable pre-dinner conversation. The sweat starts to bead even before the chef arrives to build the towering volcano of flaming onions. When you call to make reservations, tell them that you want a downstairs table.

Once you are seated at your (downstairs) table, you'll find yourself next to visitors or locals, depending upon the night, and will have some get-to-know-you time before the chefs arrive. The waiter will take your drink order and bring you the Shabu-Shabu soup and white or fried rice (we suggest the white). The soup is the one real disappointment at Kobe. It is salted as heavily as the Pacific, and the anemic beef flavor – which should be very hearty and savory – is completely overwhelmed.

Things get better once the chefs arrive. Two stand back to back in the center of the 14-seat square tables. They don't interact much with each other, saving the show for the people directly in front of them. Oil is poured and shrimp tossed onto the grill. They fling and slice with gusto, peppering their audience with silly questions and flipping shrimp tails into their air to catch in their tall hats. When it's time to add fire to the appetizer (shrimp comes free with your dinner) they splash the food with brandy and set fire to the whole thing. We once asked what kind of brandy they use, and the chef said "The cheap kind, the cheaper the better." When we checked the bottle, the second ingredient was grain alcohol. It all burns off by the time it's on your plate, and glazes the shrimp beautifully.

Once the shrimp is made and served, they make fried rice and whatever meat you've chosen. The scallops are particular favorites with us – these cooks really know how to sear them perfectly. The nuggets of tender white flesh end up perfectly crisp on the outside and just barely warm in the middle. Perfect.

The steak is very good, also, and if you upgrade to the filet, you'll be extra happy. The lobster is buttery and rich, and the opakapaka (Hawaiian pink snapper) is tender and delicately flavored. The salmon, which also holds up well on the hibachi, is delicious, tender inside and crisply seared outside.

The vegetable medley served on the side features mushrooms, onions (built into a tower and then set alight with that crazy brandy), zucchini, and bean sprouts, seasoned and set on fire just like everything else is.

The waiter brings tea to end it all, and just as your belly begins to understand what's just happened, it's time to leave. We tend to skip dessert and head to Lappert's for ice cream instead. Our only complaint about Kobe is that they haven't opened up a restaurant in South Maui. If you've got kids, a large group, or just like meeting new people while eating good food, Kobe is a good choice.

Hours: Nightly, 5:30pm-10pm, cocktails from 5pm,
Sushi Bar 5:30pm-11:30pm ***Meals:*** Dinner
Cost: $15 - $50 (depending upon what you order)
Known For: Japanese, Seafood, Steak, Sushi ***Kid-Friendly:*** Yes
Alcohol: Yes, full bar ***Website:*** www.kobemaui.com
Reservations: Highly recommended, and on some nights, required.
Credit Cards: All Major

Location: West Maui, Lahaina 136 Dickenson St. ***808-667-5555***
How to Find: behind the historic Baldwin house.
Parking: Validated parking behind Baldwin house, limited parking behind Kobe.

Top Sushi

KOISO SUSHI BAR

Ambience: 16 *Food:* 23
Service: 23 *Value:* 21
Overall: 83

You won't find Koiso in any other guide, and most locals wouldn't reveal this dining secret for fear of being crowded out of their regular sushi fix. But we're not afraid. Not everyone will want to eat here, but true sushi fanatics deserve to find out about it.

Tucked into the back of the Dolphin Plaza next to a really bad Mexican joint is the best sushi on the island served in a hole in the wall plastered with family photos and old Kirin posters.

The chef/owner, Hiro-san, is a Master Sushi Chef, and his skill with a knife is a wonder to behold. He flies his fish in from Japan via Oahu daily and works with locals to bring only the best to his sushi bar. At most, this place seats fourteen when packed.

The menu is spare and posted in handwriting on a dry erase board. The fish is all displayed in the bar, of course, and you can always point. You won't find anything like a fancy-upside-down-dragon-69-butterfly-Philadelphia-cream-cheese roll. This is strictly standards from Japan.

We particularly like the Molokai shrimp - get the shrimp as sushi, then have him bake the heads (yes!) until they're crunchy. This delicacy is amazing. We also order the eel with avocado, the spicy tuna (he uses sashimi grade tuna - no leftover bits), and the scallops. And don't let us forget to mention the soft and salty uni. We often just put ourselves in his capable hands and let him feed us.

Limited sake and beer selections warm you up, as does the amazing miso soup. It's hearty and flavorful while surprisingly light. Also, order the cucumber salad so you can watch him slice the cucumbers as thin as any mandolin could.

Hiro-san can be picky about his diners, we've noticed. This little place is like his home, and we've seen him turn people away with "no room" while the three of us dining gazed in guilty concentration at our plates piled with delicacies.

We recommend visiting Hiro-san, but not if this is your first time eating sushi (go to Sansei or even Hakone for an excellent meal and enthusiastic distribution of beginner chopsticks).

If you are a true devotee of the sea, however, we have a recommendation about how to introduce yourself. Open the door slowly and step just inside, and when he looks up ask him if he has any room to seat you. Then try to look knowledgeable but deferential and wait for a response. He will most likely gesture to a chair - or if it's full, tell you how long a wait it is likely to be. You'll have to decide for yourself how long you can wait to eat, but we always do, because it's worth it.

If you're thinking reservations would guarantee a seat, desist. He only makes reservations for regulars.

This may all sound very cloak and dagger to you, and perhaps we're exaggerating a little. In short, we're saying that Hiro-san is a very nice man, but his training and skill should be treated with respect. We pass these tips on because we've seen what works and what doesn't. Be nice, bow your head to a true master, and eat your heart out.

Hours: 6pm-9pm ***Meals:*** Dinner ***Cost:*** $10-$50
Known For: Sushi ***Credit Cards:*** MC, VS

Location: South Maui, Kihei 2395 S. Kihei Rd. ***808-875-8258***
How to Find: In the back of Dolphin Plaza, near Boss Frog's
Parking: Parking lot.

Top Donut
KRISPY KREME

We thought long and hard about including Krispy Kreme in this guide, but we finally decided to, for several reasons.

1. It's the best donut on an island not known for donuts.

2. It's the only location in the islands - people fly to Maui from Oahu to buy donuts for special events and staff meetings.

3. You can't miss it - it's the first restaurant you see as you leave the airport. And if you know about it ahead of time, you can plan to go if you see the "Hot Now" sign lit (we always seem to end up at Costco - just across the street - right about 5pm, when the light magically goes on. We don't know how this happens).

The question is what not to eat. Donuts are an intensely personal food. We leave it to you to decide for yourself. However, keep in mind that a glazed confection will be free to you when you come in when the sign is lit on the outside. And in our opinion, that confection is best eaten when piping hot, so the melt-in-your-mouth effect is strongest.

These freeze well, and if you are staying in a rental and have a microwave, eight seconds on high is the recommended defrosting time. We also have a friend who wraps a glazed donut in tin foil and grills it - she claims this preparation "rules." Finally, back in college at UVA, Jim was fond of something called a "grillswich": a grilled donut with a scoop of vanilla ice cream on top.

Krispy Kreme also features great coffee and the cleanest and most private restrooms on the island. A great pit stop is worth the dollar donut, right?

Hours: Sunday-Thursday, 5:30am-10pm drive thru, lobby 'til 8pm; Friday-Saturday, 5:30am-12am drive thru, lobby 'til 10
Meals: Are donuts a meal? ***Cost:*** $1/donut, unless the neon sign's on, in which case a glazed donut is free ***Kid-Friendly:*** Yes
Website: www.krispykreme.com ***Credit Cards:*** All Major

Location: Central Maui, Kahului 433 Kele St. *808-893-0883*
How to Find: Across from Costco at Hana Hwy and Dairy Rd.
Parking: Parking lot

Top Local Food

L&L HAWAIIAN BARBECUE

Ambience: 11 *Food:* 17
Service: 16 *Value:* 19
Overall: 63

Traditional Hawaiian "plate lunch" was designed to keep laborers working in the fields all day long. Today's version is still gigantic: a huge plate is loaded with two mountainous scoops of rice, a round of macaroni salad, and enough hot barbecue to feed a family of four.

As different Asian cultures arrived on the islands, their cuisines were also incorporated into the plate lunch. L & L is the island's favorite for plate lunches, and with good reason. The solid good food - if a little heavy - combined with low prices makes it a must-try.

Try the barbecue chicken or the beef short ribs with the spicy and sweet house barbecue sauce. The breaded chicken is good, with a katsu dipping sauce. Order a "mini" plate to get only one serving of rice rather than two.

Kids are guaranteed to love L & L, and the food court and shopping mall locations make it an easy, informal dining experience.

With franchise locations in every Western state (and now even one in New York City), this long-time local favorite may already be familiar to you. If not, definitely stop in for some cheap and tasty barbecue.

Hours: Daily, 9:30am-9pm ***Meals:*** Lunch, Dinner ***Cost:*** \$5-\$12
Known For: Barbecue, Local ***Kid-Friendly:*** Yes.
Website: www.hawaiianbarbecue.com ***Credit Cards:*** MC, VS

Location: Central Maui, Kahului Maui Marketplace, 270 Dairy Rd. (in food court near Sports Authority), Kahului ***808-873-0323***

Location: West Maui, Lahaina Lahaina Cannery Mall, 1221 Honoapiilani Hwy., Lahaina ***808-661-9888***

Location: Central Maui, Wailuku 790 Eha St., Wailuku ***808-242-1380***

Location: South Maui, Kihei Safeway Shopping Plaza, 247 Piikea Ave., Kihei ***808-875-8898***

Top Romantic Lahaina View

LAHAINA STORE GRILLE & OYSTER BAR

Ambience: 22 ***Food:*** 19
Service: 19 ***Value:*** 20
Overall: 80

We fell in love with this restaurant the moment we stepped foot inside. Located on the top floor and rooftop of the historic Lahaina Store building, the interior is elegant, open, and cries out for a special celebration.

Sit in the expansive dining room or ask for rooftop seating (call ahead for reservations around sunset) and head up to one of the most amazing views on Maui.

The food matches the restaurant in attention to detail and elegance. If you're an oyster fan, go for it - the 47-foot oyster bar is stocked with delicacies from all over the world - but be aware that none of them are local, although they are as fresh as you can get in most places.

We also recommend the homemade mozzarella in the Kula tomato caprese salad. The balsamic dressing is perfect, and the whole salad is refreshing. There's a range of surf and turf options, none of which have disappointed us. We want to call your attention in particular to the caramelized sea scallops for dinner and the seawater-soaked free range chicken. If you're looking for something heartier, the grilled tenderloin is a favorite.

The lobster ravioli are made in house, and it is on both lunch and dinner menus, which is convenient. The service is attentive and quick. While the desserts look tempting, we find the cheesecake not as "authentic New York" as the server promises. We'd skip it in favor of a cone at Lappert's later on after you hit the galleries.

Note: We have had some mixed reviews from readers over this restaurant. Some diners have found tough steak and bad service. Others have written to tell us how dead on our review is. We've always had a good time and great food, but fair warning, we have had some complaints.

Hours: Daily, 11am-10pm (bar and 47 foot oyster bar open until midnight), roof deck opens at 5:30. Nightly, 5:30pm - 10pm for dinner. Nightly, cocktails from 5pm. Nightly, Sushi Bar 5:30pm - 11:30pm.
Meals: Lunch, Dinner ***Cost:*** \$8-\$50 ***Known For:*** Seafood, Steak
Kid-Friendly: Yes ***View:*** Gorgeous view of Lahaina Harbor and Lanai, especially from the roof at sunset. ***Alcohol:*** Yes, full bar
Website: www.lahainastoregrille.net ***Reservations:*** Highly recommended, and on some nights, required. ***Credit Cards:*** All Major

Location: West Maui, Lahaina 744 Front St. ***808-661-9090***
How to Find: Across from the seawall, right in the middle of the block.
Parking: Park in lots behind restaurant (enter from Dickenson St.) Or park on street or nearby lot.

Top Ice Cream

LAPPERT'S

Lappert's is our local super-premium ice cream. The exotic flavorings are uniquely Hawaiian, and locals and tourists alike lap them up. Guava, macadamia nuts, pineapples, mangos, Kona coffee, and coconuts are just a few of the surprises.

They make their own waffle cones while you watch, and will dip them in chocolate and other decadent toppings at your request.

Try Kauai Pie, a combination of Kona coffee ice cream, macadamia nuts, coconut and chocolate fudge. It's entirely delicious. There are over 100 flavors - although stores don't carry all of those.

Although you probably should take advantage of the Hawaiian flavors, we like the "plain" flavors just as well as the more exotic combinations. The mint chocolate chip, for example, is very good. For something lighter, try Tutu's Picnic, all the sorbets swirled together. Delicious.

We can almost guarantee that you'll be more satisfied with their $3+ cone than most restaurants' dessert menus.

Known For: Ice Cream ***Cost:*** $3.50 ***Kid Friendly:*** Yes
Website: www.lapperts.com ***Credit Cards:*** MC, VS

Location: South Maui, Wailea Shops at Wailea, Wailea Alanui Dr.

Location: South Maui, Kihei Rainbow Plaza on S. Kihei Rd.

Location: West Maui, Lahaina 693 Front St.

Top Dive Bar

LIFE'S A BEACH

Ambience: 15 ***Food:*** 15
Service: 18 ***Value:*** 22
Overall: 70

Last year a friend took a belated Maui honeymoon with her husband and asked us for a "good dive bar." They met in one ten years ago and wanted to relive the memories for a few hours. We sent them to Life's A Beach.

With sand on the floor in the small outdoor seating area, neon-lit palm trees, live music you can hear in the park across the street, several pool tables, and a 4-7pm happy hour featuring cheap (and very good) mai tais, you can't get more Maui dive than this. Come to watch the cute girls, hang out, and kick back. The food is definitely not the point . . . but it's inexpensive enough to not interfere with your enjoyment. If a party bar is your thing, this is the place to be.

Hours: Daily 11-2am ***Meals:*** Lunch, Dinner ***Cost:*** $5-15
Known For: Mexican ***Alcohol:*** Yes, full bar, great happy hour
Website: www.mauibars.com ***Credit Cards:*** All Major

Location: South Maui, Kihei 1913 S. Kihei Rd. ***808-891-8010***
How to Find: next to Foodland ***Parking:*** Kalama Villages parking lot

Top Steak
LONGHI'S

Ambience: 21 *Food:* 22
Service: 20 *Value:* 20
Overall: 83

Bob Longhi opened his first location in Lahaina nearly 30 years ago, and we're glad he did (the Wailea location in the Shops is also a welcome addition to South Maui).

Longhi's can be relied upon for a great meal in a comfortable, open atmosphere. The waiters are trained heavily about the food, the preparations, and what's available in the kitchen that particular day - you can rely on their knowledge to steer you right.

The food is nearly all served family style. That's why it's kind of fun to sit down, check things over on the extensive menu, then tell your waiter what kind of meal you're in the mood for and let them guide your selections.

Pastas aren't listed on the menu, because they are considered a per order dish. Most familiar shaped pastas are available. They are handmade and sauced any way you like them.

We think Longhi's does the best steak on the island (better than Ruth's Chris, and with a better location than Makawao Steak House). Tender, flavorful, and served in delicious wine and/or butter sauces, the beef here is of the highest order. For some cuts they serve the highest quality Prime on the island.

Shrimp Longhi is the signature dish, and it's fantastic, rich and pillowy. The shrimp is served on toast points with a rich butter wine sauce and tomatoes perched atop.

The lamb is tender and flavorful, grilled and served with a raspberry sauce that always turns our heads.

The free pizza and jalapeno breads they serve hot as you sit down are ellent in that guilty way. They are not shy about cheese or olive oil . . . but we've never seen a diner turn away from a plate of these babies.

The salads are all tasty and hearty. Our favorite is the endive salad with caramelized macadamia nuts, Italian Gorgonzola cheese and honey-scallion-mint vinaigrette.

Many people love Longhi's for breakfast, and we're in agreement. They are the only restaurant on island with actual fresh-squeezed orange juice, they have excellent coffee served in French presses, and the food is excellent. It's not cheap, but it's good. The presentation leaves something to be desired, but the portions are big and you won't leave hungry.

This is one of our favorite restaurants on the island, and we highly recommend you visit.

Hours: Daily, 7:30am-10pm ***Meals:*** Breakfast, Lunch, Dinner
Cost: \$20-\$50 ***Known For:*** Pasta, Seafood, Steaks
Kid-Friendly: Yes ***Alcohol:*** Yes, full bar ***Website:*** www.longhi-maui.com
Reservations: Recommended ***Credit Cards:*** All Major

Location: West Maui, Lahaina 888 Front St. ***808-667-2286***
Parking: Street, lots nearby ***View:*** Lahaina seawall and harbor

Location: South Maui, Wailea 3750 Wailea Alanui, (Shops at Wailea) Wailea
Parking: Mall Parking Lot ***808-891-8883***

LULU'S

Ambience: 19 ***Food:*** 18
Service: 18 ***Value:*** 20
Overall: 75

Lulu's is a scene, and it's a good one. The servers are all very cute. The bar is the central feature with lots of beers on tap, and there is lots of "harbor" paraphernalia on the walls. It's the kind of place that would be a dive if it weren't so hopping with locals, visitors, and at certain times of the day, families.

On the second floor of a building in Kalama Village you'll find a big central bar, a huge lanai for seating with good views during sunset, and pool tables.

The food is pretty good. Try the popcorn shrimp, and the nachos piled high - they may not be that exciting, but they are good bar snacks.

Their burgers especially satisfy, even though they all have too-cute names. There's a peanut butter burger called the Dick Butkus that's worth trying - the sweet peanut taste actually complements beef nicely.

The Loco Moco is also a favorite. You'll see this dish in many places - the original version is rice covered in ground beef, gravy, and topped with two eggs over easy. The Lulu's burger is hearty for sure.

Lulu's is a good bet when you're feeling a little rowdy and want a bar scene, or when you have a large group and want to make sure everyone's happy. Kids like it, and the pool tables in the back are a plus, as are the live music and the occasional eating contest.

Hours: 11am-1:30am daily ***Meals:*** Lunch, Dinner ***Cost:*** $7-$20
Known For: Burgers, Sandwiches ***View:*** Good for sunset, also good for people-watching ***Kid-friendly:*** Yes, there's a large open lanai area away from the bar ***Alcohol:*** Yes, full bar.
Website: www.lulusmaui.com ***Reservations:*** Not required
Credit Cards: All Major

Location: South Maui, Kihei 1945 S. Kihei Rd. ***808-879-9944***
How to Find: In the Kalama Village Shopping Center, second floor in the back building. Turn at the 76 Gas Station, look for the rail hung with boat buoys and life rings ***Parking:*** In the Kalama Village lot.

Top Steak House

MAKAWAO STEAK HOUSE

Ambience: 19 ***Food:*** 20
Service: 22 ***Value:*** 20
Overall: 81

Makawao is a cowboy town, and this is a cowboy restaurant. Upcountry locals consider this a standard, and you'll find a good mix of native Hawaiian, Haole, and a few visitors in this friendly, cozy restaurant on Makawao's main drag.

There are no surprises here, but we don't want any at a steakhouse - we come here when we want a really good steak.

The prime rib is very good. It sprawls across your plate and promises excellent leftovers (if you have a hotel refrigerator, it makes great sandwiches the next day). The tenderloin and filet are also favorites.

The salad bar is exactly what we want it to be in a restaurant like this - all the basics including iceberg lettuce, shaved carrots, sliced cucumbers, croutons, and raisins.

The wait staff is uniformly friendly, knowledgeable, and "real." You'll feel like you're dining in a fine steakhouse circa 1975.

It's fun to sit in the lounge, and you can also eat there, if you don't want to wait for a table. The wood-burning fireplace is actually needed in the winter when our thin blood adjusts to the evening cool.

The fresh fish preparations are all good, as is the chicken, but we recommend eating fish elsewhere and ordering steak here. The desserts are rich, but you'll probably be full up on beef.

If you are considering Ruth's Chris for an evening out, we urge you to think of Makawao Steak House instead. We think the food is just as good at much better prices, and you get the added advantage of taking a drive through beautiful country and hanging with real Maui-ans. And on the way home, you get to see the stars, big, bright, and beautiful in the cool crisp night air at 1600 feet above sea level.

In any case, tip your waitress well and tip your hat on the way out.

Hours: Nightly 5:30-9:30pm, closed Mondays ***Meals:*** Dinner
Cost: $15-$35 ***Known For:*** Steak ***View:*** Great for local people-watching. This is where the upcountry cowboys eat. ***Kid-friendly:*** Yes.
Alcohol: Yes, full bar ***Reservations:*** Recommended
Credit Cards: MC, VS

Location: Upcountry, Makawao 3612 Baldwin Ave. ***808-572-8711***
How to Find: About a block before the intersection with Makawao Ave. when you approach from Pa'ia. Look for an old (1927) house that's been lovingly restored. ***Parking:*** Street.

MAKAWAO SUSHI & DELI

Ambience: 16 ***Food:*** 18
Service: 17 ***Value:*** 18
Overall: 69

Makawao is the closest we get to a college town aesthetic on Maui. The stores are all independent and locally owned, and there are a lot of them – telling us that people come to spend money in town.

The result for us foodies? A limited selection (there aren't enough people living upcountry, or enough money in their pockets, to do haute cuisine), but good quality (see Casanova and Makawao Steak House). We want to reveal an often overlooked gem of an establishment: Makawao Sushi and Deli.

Perched in a narrow storefront next to the General Store on Baldwin Ave., you'll find a cheerful room decorated with local art and selling a select few local food items. The ice cream counter and coffee bar dominates the front, and we urge you to have some coffee, because it is very strong but well-balanced. And if you like milkshakes, they do an excellent version, thick and creamy and blended from the very good local Roselani ice cream brand. Pastries are good, especially the brownies, and their sandwiches are basic but well-executed. You can sit at tall tables to eat, or they'll make it to go.

Tucked in the back of the store is the sushi bar with just a few seats waiting. The chef is competent and quick with a knife – he's no Hiro-san (see Koiso), but he's better than most. We advise you skip the miso (flavorless, unless you count "extremely salty" as a flavor) and go straight for the fish. Be ready to talk to the locals sitting at the counter with you, because they'll want to know all about you.

In short, if we're craving sushi and find ourselves upcountry, this is where we stop. We enter, go straight to the back, order our sushi, enjoy it, and then stop for ice cream or coffee on the way out. Simple, straightforward, and a decent value.

Hours: 7am-9pm ***Meals:*** Lunch, Dinner ***Cost:*** $5-15
Known For: Ice Cream, Sandwiches, Sushi
Kid-Friendly: Yes ***Credit Cards:*** MC, VS

Location: Upcountry, Makawao 3647 Baldwin Ave. ***808-573-9044***
How to Find: Baldwin Ave. next to the General Store. ***Parking:*** Street

MA'ALAEA GRILL

Ambience: 21 ***Food:*** 19
Service: 19 ***Value:*** 20
Overall: 79

This restaurant features a great view of the Ma'alaea Harbor. During whale season, you are likely to spot them while dining - and if you are very lucky, you'll see them breaching.

Ma'alaea Grill is one of our favorite places for lunch. The atmosphere and the quality of food combined with the reasonable prices make it a real bargain for a nice mid-day meal. And it's right next door to the Ocean Center as well as the harbor where many of the snorkel boat trips depart.

Choose from a wide selection of pasta, sandwiches, burgers, and fish. At lunch, try the chicken curry salad - tender and flavorful - or the crab sandwich.

At dinner, go for the appetizers – you might not make it to the main course menu with dishes like the grilled seafood tower calling your name. In terms of dinner entrees, we are fans of the duckling as well as the kiawe grilled New York steaks. Every entrée comes with a nice dinner salad and (for Maui) tasty dinner rolls.

Though there is outdoor seating opt for the inside – the harbor weather is often too windy to make for an enjoyable meal.

If you are heading out on a whale watch, snorkel trip, or visiting the aquarium, we think this is your best bet for lunch in Ma'alaea (unless you want to walk down to Buzz's and try their outrageous prawns). If you're wondering if this is a better choice than Blue Marlin, it is.

Hours: Daily 10:30am-9pm, lunch only on Mondays ***Meals:*** Lunch, Dinner
Cost: $15-$35 ***Known For:*** Pasta, Salads, Sandwiches, Seafood, Steak
View: Amazing views of the harbor, and you can often see whales breeching while you dine ***Kid-friendly:*** Yes. ***Alcohol:*** Yes, full bar.
Website: www.cafeoleirestaurants.com/thegrill
Reservations: Recommended ***Credit Cards:*** All Major

Location: Central Maui, Ma'alaea Harbor 300 Ma'alaea Rd ***808-243-2206***
How to Find: Past the Ocean Center and all the way in the back of the little village area ***Parking:*** Ma'alaea Harbor parking lot

Top Seafood
Top Ma'alaea Restaurant
MA'ALAEA WATERFRONT RESTAURANT

Ambience: 21 *Food:* 23
Service: 22 *Value:* 21
Overall: 87

If the Waterfront (most people drop "Ma'alaea" when referring to this restaurant) had more convenient parking and a sunset view, it would easily rival Mama's Fish House for best overall dining experience on Maui. It already rivals that behemoth in food, service, and wine list.

Waterfront is a true local's favorite. The hand-stenciled walls and round booths inside are retro-Hawaiiana-kitschy, but outside seating on the lanai is beautiful.

The view is superb. You'll see and hear the waves coming in from Ma'alaea Harbor, whales cavorting in season, and dolphins spinning about most of the time. The southern exposure means you miss a direct sunset view, but it's lovely nonetheless.

The food is, to put it plainly, fabulous.

If you like Caesar salad, then you will LOVE the table-side preparation. At $9 per person it can seem steep, but it is absolutely worth it. The perfect balance of anchovies, garlic, mustard, cheese, croutons, and romaine lettuce - all made while you watch. If you go more than once (and many people do), and liked the way your Caesar was prepared, ask for the same waiter - because every waiter makes the same recipe just a tad differently.

We also love the Kula onion soup. Kula onions are sweet, but they don't overpower the savory combination of beef and chicken stock with lots of garlic, thyme, and parmesan.

All fish is bought that day, often off the fisherman's boat in the harbor right outside the door. Depending upon availability, you will choose from ahi, salmon, hapu'u, lehi, mahi mahi, monchong, onaga, ono, opah, opakapaka, papio, buta papio, and striped marlin.

Once you choose your fish, then you choose the preparation - from light and basic white wine preparations to complex Pacific Rim preparations. Something will certainly appeal to you, and the black-tie waiters are unfailingly helpful in advising you on fish and preparations.

If they have it, we love the hapu'u (a Hawaiian sea bass, mild and delicate) in the southwestern preparation (salsa, peppers, black beans, smoked avocado, chili pepper, and cilantro butter).

We also like the Opakapaka En Bastille. Wrapped in fresh angel hair potato pasta, then sautéed and topped with fresh scallions, mushrooms, and tomatoes and served with meunière sauce, this is a head turner. As in, everyone at the table next to you will turn their head to see which dish is making you groan with delight.

With one of the most extensive wine lists on Maui and exceptional lava flows (strawberry pina coladas), you will not be lacking for libations.

The desserts are good, but we haven't found anything there to scream about. We usually order the salad, some fish, and skip dessert.

This is a very special restaurant. If you want to avoid the "touristy" feel of Mama's, and can live without a sunset view, for the same prices you can have just as good a meal at Waterfront with service to match.

Hours: Daily, 5pm-10pm (last seating: 8:30pm) ***Meals:*** Dinner
Cost: $20-$50 ***Known For:*** Salads, Seafood
View: Unusual view of the harbor, you can see the West Maui Mountains and Haleakala. ***Kid-friendly:*** Yes, although we rarely see them here.
Alcohol: Yes, full bar and a great wine list.
Website: www.waterfrontrestaurant.net
Reservations: Highly Recommended ***Credit Cards:*** All Major

Location: Central Maui, Ma'alaea 50 Hauoli St. ***808-244-9028***
How to Find: From the highway, turn left on Kapoli St., as if you were going to the Ocean Center. Turn right onto Ma'alaea Rd. Turn left onto

Hauoli St. Just after the bend in the road you will see the restaurant's sign. Turn right, then right again into their limited parking lot on the upper level of the condo parking center. Park in the spots marked Waterfront, and then follow the signs around to the other side of the building and the restaurant door.

Top Tapas Bar

MALA AN OCEAN TAVERN

Ambience: 24 ***Food:*** 21
Service: 19 ***Value:*** 23
Overall: 87

A favorite of locals, tucked behind Safeway, not-quite-in-downtown Lahaina, it's easy to zip by Mala without noticing it.

But if you're "down a pint," you should stop in. This casual little ocean-side tavern with fabulous chef Mark Ellman at the helm is just the ticket when you want a light meal (or not) and a few drinks.

The tapas (small dishes) menu starts at 4:30pm everyday, but they serve a few favorites earlier for the lunchtime and happy hour crowd. Try the ahi tartare – a lovely plate of chopped ahi with capers, lemon, and red onion which is absolutely melt-in-your-mouth delicious.

We also like the crunchy calamari with aioli and addictive mojo verde. The calamari is battered in a very light panko crumb and barely deep fried – meaning that the texture stays delicate, not rubbery. The aioli and mojo verde (a kind of pesto made with cilantro or tomatillos rather than basil), is absolutely delicious – the sturdy structure to the sauce perfectly complements the fish.

The Kobe beef burger with smoked applewood bacon, caramelized onion, and blue cheese is positively decadent. The entrees are hearty, too, and our favorites are the baby back ribs over purple mashed potatoes and the flat iron steak. Also, try the Avalon seared sashimi with shiitake mushroom ginger sauce.

The restaurant is open to the ocean breezes – whether you sit out on the lanai or inside. The full bar includes great beer on tap and a good wine list. If you're not sure what to order, the servers are knowledgeable.

Service is good, and the ambiance can't be beat for making you sit back, relax, and contemplate how good life can be. If you're looking for a little out of the way spot while visiting Lahaina town, this might be the place for lunch or late afternoon drinks and a light meal. We highly recommend Mala.

Hours: Monday - Friday 11am-10pm; Saturday 9am-10pm; Sunday 9am-9pm; Saturday and Sunday Brunch Menu 9am-3pm; Happy Hour 3pm-4:30pm daily ***Meals:*** Dinner ***Cost:*** $15-$30
Known For: Burgers, Kobe Beef, Seafood, Tapas, Wine Bar
View: You can't get closer to the water than their lanai. Gorgeous view of Lahaina Harbor and Lanai. ***Kid-friendly:*** Yes
Alcohol: Yes, full bar ***Website:*** www.malaoceantavern.com
Reservations: Suggested ***Credit Cards:*** All Major

Location: West Maui, Lahaina 1307 Front St. ***808-667-9394***
How to Find: Behind the Safeway Shopping Center, right on the water.
Parking: There are few spots next to the restaurant, or park at Safeway and walk over.

Top Romantic Restaurant
Top Splurge Restaurant
MAMA'S FISH HOUSE

Ambience: 24 *Food:* 23
Service: 21 *Value:* 19
Overall: 87

This is a must go place if you want a true Hawaiian dining experience. Although it's become more crowded and "touristy" in the last year, we still love Mama's and think if you haven't been here, you might be missing out.

The menu lists scores of fresh fish and the names of the fishermen who caught them that day, and most times the location of the catch. Each fish is matched to an exquisite preparation featuring local delicacies like tropical fruit, native vegetables, seaweed, ferns, Maui onions, and roasted macadamia nuts.

The décor will bring you back to old Hawaii. The interior of the restaurant opens up in such a way that the breezes and light make this a true tropical vision. The curved lauhala-lined ceilings meet walls of split bamboo and throughout the restaurant you'll find gorgeous arrangements of tropical flowers.

This is not a particularly quiet restaurant - it's too busy and popular with families to make it so - but it is terribly romantic, and if you are dining with your sweetheart, the world will disappear for you both.

The honey bread is made fresh daily on site, and its soft texture melts in your mouth. You'll also be served a small demitasse of seafood-based soup to amuse your palate.

The servers wear Hawaiian shirts and real flowers behind their ears. The service is top notch and very attentive. Most servers have worked here for years and some have confided it's the best gig on the island for working conditions, pride in your work, and putting the kids through college.

Most meals on Maui can be had elsewhere in the world - whether it's New York, Paris, or Tokyo - but nowhere else will you find a meal and a dining experience like you will have at Mama's Fish House. It is unique in all of Hawaii, and we recommend it above all others for a true Hawaiian experience.

We would suggest you call at least a week before you want to dine to ensure you get a reservation at this very special restaurant.

If you can give up the gorgeous sunset view, but want food just as wonderful and Hawaiian, you might try Ma'alaea Waterfront. You'll spend as much, won't have as stunning a view, but may find yourself happier in the smaller restaurant.

Hours: Daily from 11am-9:30pm ***Meals:*** Lunch, Dinner ***Cost:*** $25-$32
Known For: Hawaiian, Polynesian, Seafood ***View:*** Amazing views of the beach, known to locals as Mama's Beach. Spectacular sunset dining.
Kid-friendly: Yes ***Alcohol:*** Yes, full bar, best Mai Tais on island
Website: www.mamasfishhouse.com ***Reservations:*** Required
Credit Cards: All Major

Location: North Shore, Pa'ia 799 Poho Place ***808-579-8488***
How to Find: Drive through Pa'ia on the Hana Hwy toward Hana. As you turn a sharp bend to the left, then the right, look for a boat on the left side with the sign for the restaurant. ***Parking:*** Valet

---

Top Health Food Store
Top Place to Pick Up Groceries
MANA FOODS

Ambience: 17 ***Food:*** 19
Service: 17 ***Value:*** 20
Overall: 73

This is the best health food store on the island. The cavernous, barely-reconstructed warehouse space hosts nearly everything you could want to buy for groceries, and the best produce section on the island lives here. And the prices are often lower than Safeway's.

The prepared food section is incredibly popular, and we highly recommend the bread (especially the dark Ukrainian sourdough) near the front of the store.

Buy your chocolate bars here, too – the best selection on the island is directly to the left as you enter. We actually haven't seen a better selection anywhere.

There's actually a great selection of delicacies here. We suspect that the trust-fund European surfer population has made enough requests over the years to boost the store's overall gourmet stock.

There's a separate room for cosmetics and supplements, and you can find most islanders shopping here at some point during the week (including celebrities).

If you're heading to Hana and need some groceries, this is a good place to shop. Don't miss it.

Hours: Daily 8:30am-8:30pm ***Cost:*** $3-$10
Known For: Healthy, Organic, Prepared Food, Salad Bar
Kid-friendly: Yes ***Website:*** www.manafoodsmaui.com
Credit Cards: All Major

Location: North Shore, Pa'ia 49 Baldwin Ave. ***808-579-8078***
How to Find: Turn onto Baldwin Ave. from the Hana Hwy. Mana is on the left, and their parking lot is just past them.
Parking: Parking lot just past the store. Also, street.

MANANA GARAGE

Ambience: 18 ***Food:*** 19
Service: 18 ***Value:*** 18
Overall: 73

From the gas nozzles used for door handles to the industrial glass bar, Manana Garage looks like a mechanic's shop. With lively Latin music and a sumptuous Nuevo Latin menu, it's anything but.

Cuisine ranges from South American to Cuban specialties, even including a few punches of Hawaiian and Caribbean ingredients. A great example of this is the sesame-crusted sashimi with cucumber jicama escabeche, crispy sweet potato strings, and guava chili sauce. It comes in a cocktail glass with chopsticks serving as functional décor.

A great appetizer is the Adobo BBQ duck and sweet potato quesadilla, which comes with mild green chiles.

For lunch try the Cubano Classico sandwich, which is roast pork, ham, Swiss cheese, mustard and pickle, grilled on Cuban bread and served with chile-spiced fries and tasty coleslaw. It is true to its Cuban (and Miami) roots.

And if you like cornbread, make sure you order theirs. Jalapenos (not too many!) baked into the bread subtly spice the delicious, soft meal. Add butter and honey to top it off, and you'll feel like you're mouth is melting.

If you're having trouble choosing, servers know the menu well and will enthusiastically recommend both food and drinks. We love the pineapple mojitos, for instance.

Those familiar with Latin cuisine won't be disappointed. The Manana Garage stays true to most recipes, if only adding some unique touches to the dishes to make them stand out even more.

The indoor seating is fine, but we prefer sitting outside. Kahului is busy for Maui, and you do get traffic noise, but we think the food is worth it. If you're heading for a movie at the nearby multiplex, this is a good dining option.

Hours: Sunday-Thursday, 11am-9:30pm; Friday-Saturday, 11am-10:30pm
Meals: Lunch, Dinner ***Cost:*** $15-$35 ***Known For:*** Latin American
View: None. The fence that barely keeps out the traffic noise is decorated with cute gadgets, but this is definitely not a place to go for the view.
Kid-friendly: Yes ***Alcohol:*** Yes, full bar.
Reservations: Recommended ***Credit Cards:*** All Major

Location: Central Maui, Kahului 33 Lono Ave. ***808-873-0220***
How to Find: On the corner of Lono and Ka'ahumanu. Look for the bright beach umbrellas. ***Parking:*** Parking Lot

---

Top Ravioli

MARCO'S GRILL & DELI

Ambience: 18 ***Food:*** 19
Service: 18 ***Value:*** 18
Overall: 73

Marco DeFanis, owner of Marco's Grill & Deli, brought over recipes from his Italian childhood in Philadelphia and his former establishment in New Jersey that are so authentic, you'll think you've wandered off the Parkway and into a diner.

The cornerstone of Marco's Grill is freshness – he grinds the meat himself and invests in fresh produce for all of his dishes. Everything on the menu is made in the kitchen, including the croutons and the desserts.

One of our favorite entrees is the vodka rigatoni in a pink and cream tomato sauce. You can get full- or half-sized orders. A full is enough to share with two people. Also, try adding one of their great salads, and try the basil vinaigrette.

We also love the ravioli. Stuffed with ricotta and prosciutto, these really are "pockets of love," as one New Jersey native visitor proclaimed.

Located in a high-traffic area in central Maui, Marco's gets business from all over the island. Its laidback attitude and consistently delicious meatballs and Italian sausage are what keep many locals coming back for more.

If you are looking for breakfast at any time of the day, Marco's is the place. You can get chocolate cinnamon French toast, apple cinnamon or old fashioned buttermilk pancakes. We like the classic eggs Benedict, but you can create your own specialty omelet.

We tend to visit Marco's on the way to or from the airport, when our guest either needs to refuel after a long flight or prepare for one. We're always surprised at how very good it is.

Hours: Daily 7:30am-10pm ***Meals:*** Breakfast, Lunch, Dinner ***Cost:*** $15-$35
Known For: Breakfast, Pasta, Sandwiches, Seafood, Steak
View: Hana Hwy and Dairy Rd. – big traffic! ***Kid-friendly:*** Yes.
Alcohol: Yes ***Reservations:*** Not necessary, although they can be busy.
Credit Cards: All Major

Location: Central Maui, Kahului 444 Hana Hwy ***808-877-4446***
How to Find: Kitty corner to Kmart and next to the Apple Store.
Parking: Parking Lot

MATTEO'S PIZZERIA

Ambience: 19 ***Food:*** 18
Service: 19 ***Value:*** 21
Overall: 77

While we want to have truly great pizza in South Maui, we're out of luck at Matteo's. The thin crust pizza – although a few swear by it – is disappointing compared to Flatbread in Pa'ia. The thick crust fares better, although we recommend asking them to lighten up on the cheese on both versions.

The salads are fine, nothing to write home about, but they're fresh and the servers have pepper grinders to dress them.

Sandwiches and pastas are a better bet than the pizza. If you like cheese, you'll love the lasagna, which stuffs up our sinuses for days after half a portion. We also like the basil-tomato preparation for pasta, and the vodka pink sauce.

The eggplant and chicken parmesan sandwiches are hearty and tasty.

The seating is al fresco and looks out on the golf course. It's casual, but that's what it's meant to be. This place fills a big need in Wailea: an affordable place you can bring the kids when you don't feel like paying $100/person at the resorts.

The casual order-at-the-counter-take-a-number-to-your-table service works well for families or people who just want a low-key dining experience.

Despite our initial disappointment (the owner also runs Mulligan's, see review, and the chef used to cook at Ferraro's at the Four Seasons), we've still found ourselves making regular visits to Matteo's.

Hours: 11am-10pm, Monday-Saturday ***Meals:*** Lunch, Dinner ***Cost:*** $11-$25
Known For: Pasta, Pizza, Salads ***View:*** Pretty, of the golf course and the Shops at Wailea. Not terrible for sunset. ***Kid-friendly:*** Yes
Alcohol: Yes ***Website:*** www.matteospizzeria.com
Credit Cards: DS, MC, VS

Location: South Maui, Wailea 100 Wailea Ike Drive ***808-874-1234***
How to Find: From the Piilani Hwy, follow the bend down into Wailea. The restaurant is on the left side of the divided highway, about 2/3 of the way down the hill. ***Parking:*** parking lot.

Top Ribs
Top MicroBrew
MAUI BREWING COMPANY

Ambience: 17 ***Food:*** 21
Service: 19 ***Value:*** 21
Overall: 78

It's rare that a restaurant that looks like it was decorated in the 70's, the 80's, the 90's, and today gets our high praise, but the food at Maui Brewing Company – not to mention the excellent microbrews – warrants it.

If you're visiting Maui for the first time, you may not want to sit inside a brewpub/sports bar with dark décor and muzak (played live, but still muzak) pumped through the sound system, but if you are ready for some great steaks, ribs, and mac and cheese for the kids, this is your place.

Beer is their thing, so we'll start there. We haven't tried anything we didn't like, from the clean but full-flavored Bikini Blonde Ale to the chocolate-y meal-in-a-glass Wild Hog Stout. If you want to try a little of everything before you settle on one, get the sampler for $8, six 4 oz. drafts of six different brews. Sometimes this is enough to get us through an entire meal.

A kiawe grill sits in the front of the restaurant and smells unbelievable as you walk in – this is where they grill steaks and ribs, and if you're looking for good ribs, we haven't found any better on Maui. The meat is tender and falls right off the bone due to a long slow cooking process. The sauce is our favorite on island, well-balanced between sweet, tangy, and spicy, it boldly features a not-so-secret ingredient: Crown Royal Canadian Whiskey. These are bone-sucking good.

The ribs happen to come with a red cabbage that is even better than Jim's German grandmother's: brown sugar, apples, and red cabbage braised long enough to melt together into one soft, sweet, mass of love.

A standout appetizer is the filet with peppercorn sauce. A perfectly prepared filet is sliced and fanned out with tomato slices slipped in alongside. Then a peppercorn sauce is draped over the top, the little peppercorns bursting with flavor in every bite. We also love the French onion soup - a soup we think is easy to do badly. Not here. Super sweet Maui onions are easily matched by a hearty, well-seasoned beef stock. The Swiss cheese is predictably chewy and silky, and the parmesan crouton works perfectly to blend it all together.

All beef comes from Maui Cattle Company, and while the fish is good here, we'd focus on these excellent steaks at these excellent prices. Burgers are perfect and juicy and big, and they come with your choice of toppings. The kid's menu features a mac and cheese that looks really good, and every time we visit we see kids consuming it with a look of concentrated joy on their faces.

The service is very good and very relaxed, and just as good whether you're at the bar or at a table. With excellent happy hour and late night menus (everything under $10) and TV's over the bar and the exhibition kitchen, we think you'll be happy taking a little break from palm trees and tatami mats.

Hours: 11am-midnight ***Meals:*** Lunch, Dinner, Late night pupus and sandwiches ***Cost:*** $25-35 ***Known For:*** Burgers, Ribs, Seafood, Steak ***View:*** Out of date bar, exhibition kitchen ***Kid-friendly:*** Yes ***Alcohol:*** Yes, full bar ***Website:*** www.mauibrewingco.com ***Reservations:*** Recommended ***Credit Cards:*** All Major

Location: West Maui, Lahaina 4405 Honoapiilani Hwy ***808-669-3474***
How to Find: in the Kahana Gateway Center next to Outback Steakhouse
Parking: Parking Lot

Top Coffee

MAUI COFFEE ROASTERS

Maui Coffee Roasters is touted as having the best coffee in Maui, verified by Maui News and the many locals that hang around the shop over coffee and cookies. We drink their coffee every morning, grinding it at home and brewing it fresh. We've never had better home coffee.

Maui Coffee Roasters inhabits a small storefront in a strip mall on Hana Highway, in Kahului, so it is a bit out of the way from the resorts in South or West Maui. But it's worth the stop-in for the authentic Kona coffee served both in mugs and by the pound for prices that would make the big coffee chains splutter. (You can also get a 2-pound bag of whole beans at Costco for $10, if you have your membership card with you.)

The family-owned shop offers coffee, cookies, breakfast and lunch items like veggie burgers and bagels and lox.

Hours: Monday-Friday, 7am-6pm; Saturday 8am-5pm; Sunday 8am-2:30pm
Meals: Breakfast, Lunch, Dinner ***Cost:*** $5-$12
Known For: Coffeehouse, sandwiches ***Kid-friendly:*** Yes.
Website: www.hawaiiancoffee.com ***Credit Cards:*** All Major

Location: Central Maui, Kahului 444 Hana Hwy ***808-877-2877***
How to Find: Near intersection with Dairy Rd. ***Parking:*** Parking lot

MAUI COMMUNITY COLLEGE

The Maui Community College food court is a secret lunch location worth checking out. The hours are extremely limited, but if you're coming through Kahului after riding down the volcano, it's a great place to stop for lunch. The Maui Culinary Academy trains most of the chefs and kitchen workers on the island - and this food court is where they practice their trade.

The dining room is open and airy with big round tables. Seating is communal (it's a cafeteria!) and it's a noisy atmosphere. You'll find sandwiches, sushi, a great salad bar, hot entrees, and pastries, all at student prices (average $3-7 per person). The food court is open every weekday.

If you want a fine dining experience, call for reservations at Class Act - the seated restaurant on the top floor. (Seating at the bar is also available for walk-ins.) You can watch the chefs-in-training prepare your food while you get a four-course fixed price lunch ($25/person). Each week features a different cuisine, but this restaurant is only open on Wednesdays and Fridays during the school year, so call when you get here.

Truly, this is a hidden gem. Most locals don't take advantage of the Maui Culinary Academy's cheap and delicious exhibition meals - so you'll be doubly in the know if you stop by.

Location: Central Maui, Kahului Pa'ina Building, Maui Culinary Academy, 310 W. Kaahumanu Ave. ***Food Court Phone: 808-984-3225***
How to Find: From Ka'ahumanu Ave., turn into the Maui Community College. The Culinary Academy building is located at the rear of the campus. ***Parking:*** Parking Lot
Food Court Hours: Food Court opens Monday to Friday, 11am-1pm, closed weekends, while school in session.

Class Act Exhibition Restaurant Phone: 808-984-3280
Class Act Exhibition Restaurant Hours: Wednesday, Friday, 11am-12:30pm while school is in session ***Meals:*** Lunch ***Cost:*** $3-$25
Known For: Every kind you can imagine - this is a cooking school!
View: Exhibition kitchen. ***Kid-friendly:*** Yes ***Alcohol:*** Yes at Class Act.
Website: www.mauiculinary.com - check here for scheduled menus.

Top Fish Tacos
MAUI TACOS

Ambience: 15 ***Food:*** 21
Service: 17 ***Value:*** 21
Overall: 74

Maui Tacos marries Mexican and Island cuisine using only high quality, fresh ingredients for a match made in heaven. Locals love these cheap, filling meals, and many visitors eat here several times during their visit.

The taco salad, beans, rice, lettuce, tomato, sour cream and guacamole, is a favorite. So is the hookipa burrito, and the quesadillas are always good. We also like the soft tacos. Pick your poison when it comes to protein: fish, steak, ground beef, pork or chicken.

The salsa bar features cilantro, jalapenos, pickled carrots, Maui onions, and a great selection of salsas. This is fast food at its best.

Meals: Breakfast, Lunch, Dinner ***Cost:*** $5-$11 ***Known For:*** Mexican
Kid-friendly: Yes ***Website:*** www.mauitacos.com
Credit Cards: All Major

275 Kaahumanu Ave., Queen Ka'ahumanu Center, Kahului
808-871-7726 Daily, 9:30am-9pm

2411 S. Kihei Rd., Kihei ***808-879-5005*** Daily, 9am-9pm

840 Wainee St., Lahaina ***808-661-8883***
Monday-Saturday, 9am-9pm; Sunday, 9am-8pm

5095 Napilihau St., Napili ***808-665-0222***
Monday-Saturday, 9am-9pm; Sunday, 9am-8pm

Top Margarita

MILAGROS FOOD CO.

Ambience: 18 ***Food:*** 18
Service: 18 ***Value:*** 18
Overall: 72

With a great location on the corner in Pa'ia, Milagros satisfies visitors and locals alike with great food at reasonable prices and awesome margaritas.

Look for sashimi-grade ahi in a well-priced fish sandwich. We also love the blackened ahi taquitos, in their crunchy shells. The Swiss cheese and guacamole hamburger is good, as is the baby spinach and seared blackened ahi salad. Spicy ocean garden shrimp and seafood enchiladas are also standouts.

If you're up early, the Southwestern breakfast basics like huevos rancheros and a breakfast burrito covered in enchilada sauce are a good option.

The bar is great, though small, and you'll find lots of locals indulging in the strong, delicious margaritas (try the mango). You can sit inside or outside, and either way you'll likely love the laid-back atmosphere, pleasant service, great margaritas, and consistently delicious food.

Hours: Daily 8am-11pm ***Meals:*** Breakfast, Lunch, Dinner ***Cost:*** $8-$16
Known For: Sandwiches, Seafood, Steak ***Alcohol:*** Yes, full bar.
Credit Cards: AX, MC, VS

Location: North Shore, Pa'ia 3 Baldwin Ave. ***808-579-8755***
How to Find: On the corner of Hana Hwy.
Parking: Street or lot behind restaurant.

Top Apple Streudel
Top Place for Breakfast After Sunrise on Haleakala or Before You Go to Hana

MOANA BAKERY & CAFÉ

Ambience: 18 ***Food:*** 19
Service: 17 ***Value:*** 19
Overall: 73

Off the beaten path as it is, this little gem of a restaurant is worth exploring. The giant paper art on the walls is beautiful, and while it looks a little thrown together décor wise, it's Pa'ia, and it works.

We love coming here for breakfast after we watch the sunrise on Haleakala or before we head out to Hana. While our favorite is the Eggs Benedict, everything else is good, including delicious eggs scrambled just until tender.

The kitchen uses fruits, vegetables, and herbs right from the chef's own garden to make seafood, pasta, rack of lamb, and vegetarian dishes, all served on handmade plates from local artisans.

The coffee is a must – and the espresso is very good, too. The apple strudel is the best on the island, and we often pick it up as a little treat to bring home.

With live Hawaiian music on Wednesday nights, it's a great little place. Definitely worth a stop in, and a better breakfast alternative than Charley's.

Hours: Breakfast 8am-11am, lunch 11am-3pm, brunch Saturday and Sunday 8am-3pm, dinner from 3pm-9pm ***Meals:*** Breakfast, Brunch, Lunch, Dinner ***Cost:*** $7-$20 ***Known For:*** Breakfast, Brunch, Coffee, Pasta, Sandwiches, Seafood ***Kid-friendly:*** Yes ***Alcohol:*** Yes. ***Credit Cards:*** MC, VS

Location: North Shore, Pa'ia 71 Baldwin Ave. ***808-579-9999***
How to Find: Past Mana Foods on the left as you go up Baldwin.
Parking: Street.

MOOSE MCGILLICUDDY'S

Ambience: 18 ***Food:*** 17
Service: 17 ***Value:*** 18
Overall: 70

Well-established as a Front Street party place, "the Moose" is a good choice if you're coming to Maui with friends and want a night out. Every night features a DJ and dancing, with corresponding drink specials. The happy hour prices are rock-bottom (at $1 and $2 they are low for anywhere, not just Maui), and if you're looking to see some hotties try pole dancing for the first time (or if you're one yourself), come on down.

The food is fine, for the price and the portions. We'd classify the cuisine Average American and reassure you that anything you can find at a restaurant chain like TGI Friday's is on the Moose menu, from burgers to fish to Italian to Mexican. Nothing stands out, particularly, but the burgers do have good grill marks on them.

You won't just find visitors belly up to the large central bar; we locals go to the Moose, too. The value is decent and the food good and bountiful, and you just can't beat those drink specials during happy hour. With lots of "special events," including Christmas in June, it's a yearlong fiesta that's worth visiting if you're in the mood for a loud bar scene. As their website says, you can "Feel the Heat" and "Experience the Seduction" for yourself.

Hours: 7:30-2am ***Meals:*** Breakfast, Lunch, Dinner, Happy Hour
Cost: $10-19 ***Known For:*** Breakfast, Burgers, Pasta, Sandwiches
Kid-Friendly: Yes ***Alcohol:*** Yes, full bar
Website: www.mooserestaurantgroup.com ***Credit Cards:*** All Major

Location: West Maui, Lahaina 844 Front St. ***808-667-7758***
How to Find: Second Level overlooking Front St.
Parking: Private lot (pay) or street ***View:*** Front St.

Location: South Maui, Kihei 2511 S. Kihei Rd. ***808-891-8600***

How to Find: Above Fred's Mexican Café.
Parking: Street or lot next to restaurant. ***View:*** Beach across the street

---

MULLIGAN'S ON THE BLUE/ MULLIGAN'S AT THE WHARF

Ambience: 19 ***Food:*** 18
Service: 18 ***Value:*** 18
Overall: 73

With amazing views and an open layout in their Wailea location, this Irish pub, halfway up a rolling golf course, enjoys the perfect setting. These are the only "authentic" Irish pubs on the island, and while we've enjoyed better pub food in Boston and New York, the Irish staff makes you feel right at home.

Breakfast is good, especially the corned beef hash. For lunch, traditional pub fare like burgers, sandwiches, and shepherd pie are pretty good. The fish and chips (also available at dinner) are light and crispy.

For dinner, try the porterhouse, Dublin preparation. We'd eat fish entrees somewhere else, but otherwise, the rack of lamb marinated in Guinness is excellent.

The full bar stocks both Guinness and Murphys on tap and has a decent wine list. The tropical drinks are good, and this is a great bar scene. The live music is some of the best on the island - check the local listings or call for a schedule. They also have a fixed price for dinner during the show - call for details. If you're on Maui for St. Patrick's Day it's the only place to be.

Mulligan's recently opened up the location on the Wharf in Lahaina with a similar menu and a less-than-lovely view (none). But if you're looking for a better-than-decent meal, Mulligan's is a good bet.

Location: West Maui, Lahaina 658 Front St. ***808-661-8881***
How to Find: back of the Wharf Cinema Center, across from The Banyan Tree
Parking: Validated ***Hours:*** 11am-2am ***Meals:*** Lunch, Dinner
Website: www.mulligansontheblue.com/Wharf/one.html
Cost: $15-22 ***Known For:*** Burgers, Sandwiches, Seafood, Steak
Kid-Friendly: Yes ***Alcohol:*** Yes, full bar ***Credit Cards:*** All Major

Location: South Maui, Wailea Wailea Blue Golf Course, 100 Kaukahi ***808-874-1131***
How to Find: Turn left into the golf course from Wailea Alanui Drive.
Parking: Parking Lot ***Hours:*** Daily 8am-2am
Meals: Breakfast, Lunch, Dinner
View: Spectacular at sunset – overlooks the resorts, Molokini, Kaho'olawe, and Lana'i ***Website:*** www.mulligansontheblue.com
Reservations: Recommended on weekends.
Website: www.mulligansontheblue.com

NICK'S FISHMARKET

Ambience: 23 ***Food:*** 17
Service: 17 ***Value:*** 16
Overall: 73

We hate to say this, but time after time we come to the same conclusion about the well-established Nick's: it's overrated. Our friends agree, one summing it up rather bluntly with, "It's stupid to go there."

Like the other two Tri-Star owned restaurants on Maui (Sarento's on the Beach and Son'z at the Hyatt Regency), we think that the over-the-top, almost cloying service and the unbelievably beautiful location distracts diners from the unnecessarily complex menu items.

If you're under 45, or have children who are, you may remember the song "one of these things is not like the others" from Sesame Street. Eating fish entrées at Nick's - what they are famous for - is like playing that game. There always seems to be one ingredient which just doesn't belong in the dish - and rather than a pleasant surprise, it's a blucky (as a small friend once described it) detractor.

For example, in their classic ahi with rice, edamame, wasabi beurre blanc, and avocado, the avocado takes what was a pan-Asian preparation and jolts your palate into Tex-Mex category. When scraped off, the dish becomes more palatable, but still suffers from a uniformity of soft, mushy texture and a wild swing between nearly Korean fiery hot sensation from the chili-laced edamame and an unevenly distributed wasabi within the beurre blanc sauce. They also don't slice the ahi, a detail that we simply don't understand overlooking. The fish is perfectly seared, and a great cut - so why not present it so that we can admire their handiwork? As it is, it looks like a hunk of grilled meat with that dollop of mis-matched avocado on top - not the prettiest dish, and actually rather difficult to eat because it doesn't come sliced.

The whole always seems to be lesser than the sum of its parts. The popular and highly recommended opakapaka is perfectly pan-seared. It's mounded on a heap of green parsley mashed potatoes that taste delicious on their own but don't want to be soaked through with the almost sickeningly sweet sauce. The rock shrimp that adorn the plate are delicious on their own, and the steamed veggies are crisp and flavorful, but the sugary "brown butter Mauishire" sauce overwhelms all other flavors and textures.

The calamari appetizer - which is tender with a nice crispy breading - is cloaked in a wasabi remoulade, with a spicy tomato sauce on the side. We like both sauces, but not together - and since the wasabi is already on the fish, we can't isolate the tomato. Why can't they both be served on the side? Because it won't look right, we suspect. There seems to be a rule in the kitchen that every plate begins with a sauce, and then the food is piled vertically above it. Since this style of presentation goes back to the last millennium, we're not sure it needs to be continued now. It makes eating every dish an all-or-nothing experience.

Many people comment on the dessert here, and we agree that it is often very good. The banana foster pound cake concoction is decadent, and the flaming strawberries – when they have them – are just plain delicious. But we suspect that we often order dessert to soothe our jangled nerves after the disjointed meal.

The pricey wine list is huge and wins awards for excellence. The wines by the glass are sufficiently wide-ranging to please any palette, however.

The service is so unctuous at first that we often are surprised at how slow it becomes once you place your order. And never – not once – have we had anyone check on our food while eating an entrée, even though at least three people will be in attendance throughout the meal. While they may remember our name and keep using it throughout dinner, they're likely to forget to say goodbye on our way out the door. And make sure you bring everything with you – if you leave something on the table and turn around to retrieve it, it could be gone before you're even out of sight of the restaurant. This reinforces our suspicion that this restaurant group bottom lines it with the staff and the kitchen: keep costs low and spectacle high, and move diners in and out with efficiency.

Although some love the outside tables with a gorgeous view of the landscaping at the Kea Lani, we actually prefer to sit inside the restaurant and watch the beautiful fish in the huge aquarium. This is one of the most beautiful, classy looking restaurants in Maui, and very romantic.

At the end of one particularly slow evening we eavesdropped as a just-seated couple introduced themselves to their waiter. The gentleman explained that tonight was a very special night – they were locals and lived just a few miles away, but hadn't been here in six years. However, it was the lady's fortieth birthday tonight, and they first met here at Nick's at a wedding reception, so they had decided to return for this special anniversary/

birthday celebration. That may be the only good reason we've ever heard of for dining at Nick's.

Hours: Daily 5:30-10pm ***Meals:*** Dinner ***Cost:*** $30-60
Known For: Seafood, Steak ***Kid-Friendly:*** Yes.
View: Kea Lani grounds and the ocean below, people in their bathing suits at the pool. ***Alcohol:*** Yes, full bar.
Website: www.tristarrestaurants.com/nicks/index.html
Reservations: Required ***Credit Cards:*** All Major

Location: South Maui, Wailea 4100 Wailea Alanui Dr. ***808-879-7224***
How to Find: Next to the koi pond in the Fairmont Kealani
Parking: Park in the lot directly to the left as you arrive, or valet

---

Top Lu'au

OLD LAHAINA LU'AU

Ambience: 19 ***Food:*** 19
Service: 19 ***Value:*** 19
Overall: 76

A lu'au is a traditional feast Hawaiians use to celebrate milestones like anniversaries, birthdays, weddings, and graduations. Essentially, it's a big bash thrown outdoors for everyone you know. It's hard to get invited to a local's lu'au, but Old Lahaina Lu'au is a good substitute.

There are plenty of hotel lu'aus on the island, but don't be tempted unless you just want to get drunk and stumble back to your hotel room later – the food is usually way below average and the shows are often hokey and almost condescending. Old Lahaina Lu'au has the authentic experience down – from good food to the best hula show around.

Buffet food is always chancy, but here it is reliably good. The Kalua Pig, which is barbecue roasted whole in an underground oven and literally falls off the bone in front of your eyes – is sweet, spicy, smoky, and utterly delectable. Don't skip the sweet but tangy barbecue sauce, though, because it definitely completes the flavor.

Other must-haves include the poi, the traditional Hawaiian starch, and the barbecued chicken. The last time we went, the chicken and steak were both a little overdone, but in general you can't go wrong with the all-you-can-eat feast. The price of admission includes an open bar, and the tropical drinks are delicious and strong enough to make even the most dedicated drinker happy.

The views of Lahaina harbor are some of the most romantic on the island. The staff is full of Aloha, and the tiki torches are lit when you arrive. You'll get "lei'd" upon arrival, and every need will be taken care of.

You sit at big tables with other guests, so be prepared to meet some new faces. The entertainment is the best show on the island, with fire dancing, hula dancers, and chanting of the story of Hawaii. The story, told through the sacred hula, covers migration from Polynesia through modern times, and it's treated with more reverence than we've seen elsewhere.

When we have visitors come who want to experience a lu'au, this is where we take them. Any of the food can be had anywhere else (Kalua Pig is served just about everywhere), but the experience can't. The combination of food, drink, views, and genuinely heartfelt entertainment are well-worth the cost. Kids love it!

If the idea of sitting with strangers and eating from a buffet doesn't appeal, but you still want to attend a lu'au, check out Feast at Lele with its private seating and upscale food.

Hours: Daily, in time for sunset (they'll tell you when you call to make reservations) ***Meals:*** Dinner ***Cost:*** $95 adult, $62 keiki, inclusive.
Known For: Hawaiian, Lu'au, Polynesian ***Kid-friendly:*** Yes
View: Gorgeous of Lahaina Harbor and Lana'i.
Alcohol: Yes, all-you-can-drink included with price of ticket.
Website: www.oldlahainaluau.com

Reservations: Required, although sometimes we get in if we show up and go on standby. ***Credit Cards:*** MC, VS

Location: West Maui, Lahaina 1251 Front St. ***808-667-1998***
How to Find: Behind Safeway shopping center, right on the water. Look for the Aloha girls waving you into the parking lot just before sunset.
Parking: Limited at the lu'au, or park at Safeway and walk over.

PACIFIC'O

Ambience: 22 ***Food:*** 22
Service: 19 ***Value:*** 20
Overall: 83

We love Pacific'O for lunch or late afternoon pupus and drinks. Something about sitting directly on the beach while eating elegant food just clicks. This is Chef James McDonald's more Hawaiian restaurant – sister I'O across the way is decidedly more modern in décor – but the food is just as good and just as fresh.

The fish comes in from local fishermen (and often is marched through the dining room on the way to I'O), and the produce comes all the way from their farm, O'o, in Kula on the slopes of Haleakala. These are impeccable ingredients.

We especially like the Yuzu Divers appetizer. Seared diver scallops are scooped up with arugula pesto and rolled in coconut rice and crisped up – delicious. The yuzu lime sauce provides tang and zip to the sweet fish and coconut. The tomato stack, simple as it is, is our favorite salad. Ripe tomatoes stack between slabs of buttermilk cheese and fresh basil leaves, with artichoke hearts slipped in for fun . . . then the whole stack is drizzled with roasted pepper Thai curry vinaigrette.

If you haven't gotten sick of coconut macadamia nut preparations on your fresh catch of the day, indulge in it here. The peanut coconut sauce is particularly delectable, and the tropical fruit salsa lightens things up.

But our very favorite dish is the Hapa/Hapa Tempura. Hapa means half, and that's what you get. Don't choose which fish – the chef will take the two best catches of the day and serve one of each. The sashimi is wrapped in seaweed, very quickly fried in tempura batter, and show up minutes later on a plate with an incredible lime basil sauce drizzled on one side, white miso dressing on the other. We have to keep ourselves from licking the plate.

The service can be a bit distant here – everyone seems to have an individual ritualized patter that will either work for you or won't – but unevenness in service generally does not take away from the genuine enthusiasm for food.

Many diners are so taken with the idea of eating directly on the beach that they insist on getting an outside table, but we prefer sitting on the rail for the better view. We highly recommend making reservations and specifying where you would like to sit ahead of time, since the hostesses seem to get flustered if you just walk in. While sunset views are spectacular here, we like the lunch prices – and recommend I'O for an excellent dinner with an identical view.

Hours: Daily 11:30am-4pm, 5:30-10pm ***Meals:*** Lunch, Dinner ***Cost:*** $26-38
Known For: Hawaiian Regional Cuisine, Seafood ***Kid-Friendly:*** Yes
View: Stunning, of Lahaina Harbor
Alcohol: Yes, full bar and plenty tropical drinks
Website: http://www.pacificomaui.com/ ***Reservations:*** Recommended.
Credit Cards: All Major

Location: West Maui, Lahaina 505 Front St. ***808-667-4341***
How to Find: Back of the shopping center, across from sister restaurant I'O
Parking: In the lots across the street or underneath the complex, on the street.

Top Fish Sandwich
PA'IA FISH MARKET

Ambience: 18 ***Food:*** 22
Service: 17 ***Value:*** 21
Overall: 78

We don't often insist you go to a restaurant, but we do now. It's often the first place we take first-timers, because the fish is so island-fresh and inexpensive.

Go up to the counter and order the ono burger. Ono is a tender, white fish, and the word "ono" means "delicious." You can order something else – it's all good – but if one of your party orders the ono burger (and at least one of you should), everyone else will end up wanting it. The homemade slaw, shredded cheese, and tomato slice on top of this char-grilled fish sandwich is part of what makes it all stick together into one mouth-melting, oh-my-gosh-I-can't-believe-how-good-this-is experience.

Order a basket of fries (shoestring) to share and you're good to go. Malt vinegar is the best complement to the salty-spicy seasoning on the fries, and don't worry; it's on the table when you sit down.

When you arrive the line will probably be long, because tourists and locals know this is the best fish sandwich on the island. But don't fret about not finding a seat. Somehow there is always a seat available just as they call your number. The long wooden tables and benches are designed for cafeteria style eating, but most of your neighbors will be too busy moaning with pleasure and rolling their eyes to talk.

Hours: Daily 11am-9:30pm ***Meals:*** Lunch, Dinner ***Cost:*** $8-$20
Known For: Sandwiches, Seafood ***View:*** Surfers refueling between swells.
Kid-friendly: Yes ***Credit Cards:*** DS, MC, VS

Location: North Shore, Pa'ia 110 Hana Hwy ***808-579-8030***
How to Find: On the corner of Baldwin ***Parking:*** Street, public lots.

PEGGY SUE'S

Ambience: 16 ***Food:*** 15
Service: 18 ***Value:*** 16
Overall: 65

Peggy Sue's is a 50's-style diner in a strip mall in Kihei that attracts families craving burgers after a day at the beach and bikers grabbing a cone after stopping at the Harley store. The big bikes posed outside add a stamp of authenticity to the atmosphere - as if the tattooed big boys are the modern versions of duck-tailed drop-outs.

Yes, Peggy Sue's gets the atmosphere right. There's a big jukebox and smaller versions at the tables, 50's memorabilia and pictures of Elvis and Marilyn. The waitresses dress for the occasion in cute uniforms and the grill is visible from just about any seat in the house.

Too bad they don't get the food right. Even at these prices (inexpensive for Maui), it's just not worth it. They call their 6 oz. burgers "cadillacs" and describe them as thick and juicy, but . . . they're overcooked, dried out, and nearly tasteless. They use Maui Cattle Company beef - which is really good local beef - and ruining it is a sin in our book.

Their drinks are good, and you can get real old-fashioned soda fountain treats like egg creams, cherry cokes, and lime rickeys. It's hard to go wrong with a cone of any flavor of the local Roselani ice cream, but don't be fooled (as we have been, so many times) into buying their "premium" milkshakes. A regular milkshake is made with vanilla ice cream and flavored syrup, but for $2 more you get a "premium" shake made with any other kind of ice cream. Whether you spend $5 or $7, we think you're overpaying for this too-milky concoction. Ruby's version is far superior and much thicker. And Ruby's food is also much better.

The kid's menu includes peanut butter and jelly, and that's fitting, because Peggy Sue's is a lot like a pb&j: it seems perfectly satisfying, fun to eat, and reminiscent of days gone by . . . but ends up being just spongy, empty calories slopped out and spilled along your t-shirt

Hours: Sun.-Tuesday 11am-9pm, Friday & Saturday 11am-10pm
Meals: Lunch, Dinner ***Cost:*** $9-15 ***Known For:*** Burgers, Sandwiches
Kid-Friendly: Yes, separate menu. ***Credit Cards:*** All Major

Location: South Maui, Kihei 1280 S. Kihei Rd. ***808-875-8944***
How to Find: In the Azeka Mauka Shopping Center next to Who Cut the Cheese ***Parking:*** parking lot.

PHILLY'S BLUE PLATE DINER

Ambience: 18 ***Food:*** 19
Service: 17 ***Value:*** 19
Overall: 73

Don't expect an East Coast diner - even though the Philly cheese steak is very good, this restaurant is named for the owner, who hails from more Southern climes.

The chef uses Cajun spices in most dishes, including catfish. The barbecue ribs fall off the bone and the brisket is very well flavored. The burgers are large, hand formed, and very good. The Kalua Pig sandwich on a bed of cabbage is perfectly flavored with sweet and spicy sauce.

The plain old fashioned club sandwich is very good - crisp bacon, creamy mayonnaise, ham, and turkey on whole wheat or white - all held together with long toothpicks. The Reuben is also very good. Although it's not a mile high like you'd find in New York, the quantity is adequate and the cheese is melted just right.

The French fries are worth mentioning. We thought they were homemade at first, because their flavor was so true. But the waitress told us that clean oil is the secret - that the oil is changed often, to keep all the fried foods tasting like they're supposed to.

The biscuits are worth trying if you're a biscuit fan. They're not as good as back home on the mainland, but for Hawaii, you can't get much better.

We've heard that the chef trained with Paul Prudhomme, which would explain his expertise with southern fare.

The restaurant is very open and airy, and the booths are big and comfortable. There's a large bar with flat-screen televisions, and the waitresses are friendly and knowledgeable. Definitely ask their opinion about the large menu.

Even though it's a bit out of the way, we like Philly's for lunch.

Hours: Daily 7am-9pm ***Meals:*** Brunch on weekends, Lunch, Dinner
Cost: $10-$18 ***Known For:*** Breakfast, Burgers, Sandwiches
Kid-friendly: Yes ***Alcohol:*** Yes, full bar ***Credit Cards:*** All Major

Location: South Maui, Kihei 1280 S. Kihei Rd., Azeka Makai ***808-891-2595***
How to Find: In the same plaza as the post office, back next to Ace Hardware.
Parking: Parking lot.

Top Lamb
PINEAPPLE GRILL

Ambience: 22 ***Food:*** 23
Service: 20 ***Value:*** 21
Overall: 86

The Pineapple Grill's formidable selection of expensive marketing materials touts it as a "Westside favorite." Luckily for you, this is not just spin printed on high-gloss laminated cardstock. We think it competes with Spago, Mama's, Hali'imaile General Store, and even our favorite little Waterfront for best food on Maui. Combine excellent cuisine with breathtaking views of the mountains and the ocean, and you've got a real winner.

Pineapple Grill opened in 2005, but it was built to stay. Unlike most under-capitalized Maui restaurants, it's backed by the San Diego-based Cohn Restaurant Group, with ten award-winning and money-making restaurants scattered throughout that city. The managing partner was raised on Oahu and opened the excellent Plantation Restaurant just up the hill from Pineapple Grill after a stint with Chart House and later TS' Kapalua Bar and Grill. What does all of this mean? This restaurant is run by people who know how to run restaurants. Why is that important? If you plan to have your wedding here - or even make reservations for next Christmas - the Grill is likely to still be here when you arrive.

The chef, Ryan Luckey, was lucky enough to be born on this island and cook in many of its best restaurants before taking the helm here. We like his style.

Now before you think we're too breathless, we're going to tell you the bad news. Although we respect the business background of the owners/partners, we find that the staff can seem a little stiff and deliberate, like perhaps they're being watched too closely to relax. They're unfailingly polite, and we have no complaints about the service, but there seemed (on two occasions) to be a little unease in the air. Perhaps the "fun" promised in the brochures only extends to those of us eating. Whatever the reason, it comes across as pretentious - and that's just not Maui.

Another issue - if you are seated right at the plate glass windows with the stunning ocean view, make sure you don't look too far down. The brightly lit tennis courts directly below the restaurant can prove distracting during a romantic dinner for two.

If you are lucky enough to be staying in beautiful Kapalua, you already know that this is one of the most beautiful places on the island. The name means "arms embracing the sea," and we can think of no more gorgeous view to embrace than that of Molokai in the distance at sunset with the luscious green West Maui Mountains rising above the golf course.

The elegant, glossy, expansive restaurant itself is beautiful. Large tables and comfortable rattan chairs sprawl throughout the space, which is romantic, intimate, and fun all at once. Giant flowers are painted on the vaulted ceilings in the dining rooms, and don't forget to look up as you pass or sit at the bar. You'll see sting rays and fish and blue, blue water above, as if you're looking up while snorkeling.

We love the mai tais here, so please order one if you're inclined. We'd love to do a side-by-side taste test with Mama's Fish House's version, because it's hard for us to decide which is better. They are known for their wine list, and both the chef and the managing partner are considered experts. Follow the printed pairing suggestions on the menu and you will not be disappointed. There are also many wines by the glass to choose from, so if you're driving back to the south side you might be able to indulge in one early in the meal.

It is always hard for us to choose what to eat here. The focus on locally raised vegetables, fresh fish, and island-bred beef combined with a creative approach to island cuisine makes everything look very tempting. Par-baked rolls (why don't more Maui restaurants use these delicious rolls?) help to keep the edge off the hunger while you decide.

Our very favorite entrée is a coffee-glazed rack of lamb with a veal cabernet reduction on the plate. The strong molasses/coffee flavor combined with the cushy texture of a medium rare chop is surprising and delightful. The Molokai sweet potatoes, with their deep purple flesh and nearly taffy-like texture make a perfect complement to the dish. They may be our favorite mashed potatoes on the island.

Another favorite is the pistachio-wasabi ahi. Roy Yamaguchi (Roy's) makes a similar dish, and it's definitely worth repeating here, because the flavors are just so outstanding together. The sinus-cleansing properties of wasabi are toned down and softened by the sweet flavors of the pistachios, and both provide a strong contrast to ahi's flavor. Add some coconut rice and a mushroom sauté, and we are happy diners, indeed. This also comes as a pupu (appetizer), so if you are tempted by something else, you could choose to have this for starters. You won't be disappointed.

Other good choices include the pork tenderloin and any of the fish. The menu shifts quite a bit, but you can rely on the chef's taste buds to guide you well.

The one dish that has disappointed us – and we've only had it once, so it may have been an inexperienced sous chef at fault – is the promising sounding ono with a prosciutto wrap. We were expecting a hearty meal, because ono is a steak-like fish that is often served as a burger. But the prosciutto was cut so thick that it turned into more of a brick than it should have been. The flavors were good, but somehow didn't cohere as well as necessary to really stand out.

Good dessert menus are few and far between on Maui. The air here is not good for pastry-making, and most chefs stick to local ice creams and sherbets, with a few notable exceptions. We like the pineapple and apple crisp with a serving of macadamia ice cream, and also the pineapple upside down cake. The coffee is good, too.

When you step outside, make sure you look up at the stars over the golf course.

Hours: Daily, 9am-9pm ***Meals:*** Continental Breakfast, Lunch, Afternoon Grille Menu, Dinner starts at 5:30pm. ***Cost:*** $25-$34
Known For: Seafood, Steak ***Kid-Friendly:*** Yes
View: Unbeatable. Plate glass windows and open lanai seating offer views of Lanai and the ocean or the golf course and the West Maui mountains beyond. At night, the stars are very bright in quiet Kapalua. ***Alcohol:*** Yes, full bar
Website: www.pineapplekapalua.com ***Reservations:*** Highly recommended
Credit Cards: All Major

Location: West Maui, Kapalua 200 Kapalua Drive, Kapalua Resort
808-669-9600 ***How to Find:*** Near the Bay Clubhouse and the Tennis Garden, just up from the Residences at Kapalua Bay.
Parking: parking lot outside restaurant and tennis club.

Top Lamb Pita

PITA PARADISE

Ambience: 17 *Food:* 19
Service: 18 *Value:* 20
Overall: 74

We love Pita Paradise. This little restaurant tucked away at the back of Kalama Village is the real deal. The mostly Greek menu is all good. Try the hummus platter – it's excellent.

Its gyros are a standout, made with free-range lamb and grilled perfectly. The fish is also very good, and the salad wraps are wonderful. The Greek salad is a natural. The tzatziki bread is de-lic-ious. Beer and wine are available in a limited but good selection. Their iced tea is also pretty good.

The servers are all friendly and the food comes quickly. In short, this is one of those great little restaurants that just make you happy. Superb food at good prices – and you get to eat it on a shady porch. You could eat here more than once on your visit and not be ashamed.

Hours: Daily from 11am-9:30pm ***Meals:*** Lunch, Dinner ***Cost:*** $6-$15
Known For: Mediterranean ***Kid-friendly:*** Yes
Alcohol: Yes limited beer and wine ***Credit Cards:*** MC, VS

Location: South Maui, Kihei 1913 S. Kihei Rd. ***808-875-7679***
How to Find: In Kalama Village, tucked in the back near the Tiki Lounge
Parking: Parking Lot

Top Kapalua Restaurant
PLANTATION HOUSE

Ambience: 23 ***Food:*** 21
Service: 20 ***Value:*** 22
Overall: 86

The Plantation House is situated at about 200-feet above sea level, and is our favorite place in West Maui to get a very good meal with a mind-blowing view.

"Mind-blowing" doesn't really do the sight justice. The rolling slope of the golf green dominates the foreground, while the ramrod-straight ironwood trees march down the spine of the mountain to the blue Pacific pounding at the Kapalua shores below. Molokai's dramatic profile is in the background, and the sun and clouds all do impressive tricks for your eye. You're high above the highway, but it is almost completely eclipsed by the greenery, lending the pleasant illusion that you are one of the privileged few who make a home in rural Kapalua.

In other words, make a dinner reservation ahead of time and specify a window table. Bring a sweater if you get chilled easily, as the evenings can be cool enough for them to light their fireplace in the center of the restaurant.

Plantation House is the sister restaurant to SeaWatch, one of our favorite South Maui spots, and the menu is virtually identical. This is a good thing, because we find the golf clubhouse prices a great value.

The excellent and reasonably-priced breakfasts make this a great alternative to the long lines at The Gazebo in Napili. And best of all, you can order breakfast *and* lunch from opening until the afternoon closing - which is very convenient for early lunches or late breakfasts.

We like every one of their several eggs benedict - excellent - and also the spinach and cheese omelet. We also like the Molokai sweet bread French toast with bananas. Mimosas are delicious.

For lunch, we like the Caesar salad with blackened Hawaiian fish. We also like the rosemary-garlic chicken breast sandwich. The burgers are wonderful, and at $9 – a real bargain. But our favorite is probably the upcountry spinach salad with Cajun ahi, if they have it on the menu. They really know how to do fish here, and the bed of crisp local spinach is the perfect place to showcase ahi's tender, steak-y goodness.

At dinner, we highly recommend any of the fish preparations – while there are other places to eat excellent fish on Maui, this view nearly demands that you have stellar seafood to reinforce the over-the-top Hawaiian experience. Plus, the chef has great preparations.

Listen to the waiters as they describe the daily specials (everything depends on what is available that day) and ask lots of questions about the dishes. Your trust in their recommendations will be well-rewarded. Our very favorite preparation remains the Mediterranean. The daily fish is coated with a crust of sweet Maui onions and spicy, hearty mustard, served over Maui onions roasted until the sugar is completely caramelized. Fried caper sauce is ladled over the fish, lending the exact right note of fiery snap and crunch to this melt-in-your mouth concoction.

A glass of wine from their *Wine Spectator* Award-winning list or their excellent mai tai could be in order – as well as a visit from a television crew. Plantation House is an ideal location for shooting Hawaiian dining excellence, and we've even seen Rachael Ray's crew. This is one of our favorite Maui restaurants because of the excellent value for the great food, incredible views, and engaging service (a friend once had her white napkin discreetly replaced with a black napkin to match her dress).

Hours: Open daily, Breakfast & Lunch: 8am-3pm; Dinner: 5:30pm
Meals: Breakfast, Lunch, Dinner ***Cost:*** Lunch: $7-17; Dinner: $20-30
Known For: Breakfast, Burgers, Sandwiches, Seafood, Steak
Kid-Friendly: Yes, kid's menu ***View:*** You will drool – the golf course, Kapalua shores, the ocean, and Molokai beyond ***Alcohol:*** Yes, full bar.
Website: www.theplantationhouse.com ***Reservations:*** Recommended
Credit Cards: All Major

Location: North Maui, Kapalua 2000 Plantation Club Dr. ***808-669-6299***

How to Find: Turn Mauka (mountainside) from the Honoapiilani into the Plantation Golf Course ***Parking:*** Parking lot.

PRINCE COURT

Ambience: 20 ***Food:*** 19
Service: 19 ***Value:*** 19
Overall: 77

Driving out to Makena for a Sunday Brunch at the Maui Prince is a real treat whether you live here or are just visiting. Champagne, coffee, and juice are served at the table by the wait staff. The food is all served buffet style. The spread is dazzling.

We advise browsing every table before you begin. The desserts will catch your eye first because they're near the hostess station. The carrot cake is delicious, and the key lime pie is tart-sweet in a perfect balance.

We like to start with the sushi table and work our way around to the salads. Fresh fish and smoked fish piled high, several gourmet cheeses, crackers, and rolls and bread are piled high. We'd focus on the fish, however, and skip the so-so rolls.

Meanwhile, the hot bar will have chicken, pastas, and of course breakfast items. We'd skip the scrambled eggs and go get an omelet made at the design-your-own station.

Prime rib, turkey, and ham are sliced in front of your eyes. And then there's cereals, oatmeal, pancakes, French toast . . . it's overwhelming.

The views are dazzling and the isolated Makena location with the beautiful Maui Crown Prince courtyard setting makes this a really special meal. If you like champagne, it's a great deal.

The Maui Crown is no longer the best resort on the island, but it's located in Makena, our idea of heaven. Just past Wailea and on the way to La Perouse and the lava fields, it's worth the trip.

Hours: Sunday Brunch: 9am-1pm ***Meals:*** Brunch
Cost: $44.95, $23.95 for keiki ***Known For:*** Breakfast, Brunch, Buffet
View: Absolutely beautiful. Makena has peaceful, beautiful views of Molokini, Kaho'olawe, and Lana'i. ***Kid-friendly:*** Yes ***Alcohol:*** Yes
Website: www.princeresortshawaii.com ***Reservations:*** Required
Credit Cards: All Major

Location: South Maui, Makena Maui Prince, Wailea Alanui ***808-875-5888***
How to Find: Drive through Wailea toward La Perouse Bay. The Maui Prince is on the right. ***Parking:*** Parking Lot

---

Top Japanese Restaurant

RESTAURANT TAIKO

Ambience: 24 ***Food:*** 22
Service: 22 ***Value:*** 21
Overall: 89

If you are wishing the crowds would disappear for a while, we suggest you point the nose of your car to the Diamond Hawaii Resort in Wailea for a serene Japanese getaway. You will find a luscious, meticulously prepared Japanese meal at the exceptionally fine Restaurant Taiko.

The Diamond Resort is Japanese-owned but thoroughly Aloha. It slips down Haleakala in golf villas, lush greenways, and soothing water features. The main building sits at the top of the landscape, built into the side of the mountain like a chalet. The entrance is framed by a large water feature that flows underneath the building in a series of waterfalls. Well-stocked with koi in nearly every pool you pass, it creates a dramatic centerpiece for the resort.

The menu lists all the usual sushi suspects, including salmon, snapper, ahi, clam, octopus, squid, mackerel, shrimp, sea urchin, and oysters. Rolls include spicy tuna, shrimp tempura, soft-shell crab, and some fancier versions, too. The Rainbow Roll features tuna, snapper, yellowtail, smoked salmon, unagi, avocado, squid, and tobiko wrapped tightly and resting like a fortress tower placed on its side. Another favorite includes sirloin steak, crab, cucumber, avocado, and wasabi in a creation called the Black & Blue Roll. The sushi is perfectly cut, beautifully and carefully plated, and fresh enough that the fish melts on your tongue in a blur of sweet ocean flavor.

Entrees range from sirloin in a light, zingy ginger sauce to fresh fish in a spicy, dynamite preparation. Lobster tail is delicious sautéed in butter, and pasta dishes featuring mushrooms and leeks belie the original chef's French training. You can even hibachi at your table, searing your own beef, fish, or lobster on a little flaming grill until it is done just as you like it.

Our very favorite items are listed as "Complete Japanese Meals," For less than $40 you get the main dish, rice, a rich, hearty, deeply flavored miso soup, and salty Japanese pickles – making this one of the best values on the island.

Try the Chirashi, or scattered sushi, meal. Tender slices of the best sashimi are laid over a large bowl of white rice. The chef chooses the cut and the fish for you, and each piece tastes like a little surprise gift.

Other complete meals feature salmon, pork tenderloin, or black cod. The shrimp and vegetable tempura are another favorite – the tempura is so light the vegetables nearly float off the plate.

The kid's menu is enough to satisfy any child not yet in love with sushi: deep-fried chicken strips, panko shrimp, or a hamburger, served with macaroni salad and rice.

The wine list is very nice, and they have wonderful sakes to explore. The servers are uniformly pleasant, efficient, and unobtrusive, and they will carefully advise you on every aspect of the menu.

One of our favorite touches is the beautiful wooden trays used to serve. These and the three tiered wood carts used to carry the trays from kitchen to table are beautiful but serviceably simple, and somehow reflective of the overall aesthetic at work in the ambience.

The restaurant itself is on a lower floor in the hotel, and the central water feature flows directly under the wood floor. The room is long and three-stories tall. The stone walls, massive beamed ceilings, floor to ceiling windows folded back to allow the evening breeze, long spare tables and elegant straight-backed chairs give this space a nearly monastic feel. We like to say it's a cathedral dedicated to spiritually uplifting food.

The tables are lit individually by halogen lamps (the one unattractive feature; why can't they use a softer light?), so each table sits in its own little pool of light. With the tables set far apart from each other, the restaurant is positively tranquil compared to many others on Maui.

The serenity inside is in marked contrast to the riot of Hawaiian color outside. The view from this high on the mountain is positively breathtaking. Molokini's quarter moon slots neatly into Kaho'olawe's red expanse and if it's sunset, the sky is the same color. No beach view - you're too high for that - but the green of the golf course and the Wailea resorts below create a lush foreground for the ocean's pacific glory.

The gorgeous views, lovingly prepared and executed food, civilized and private atmosphere, and gentle service all make this one of the most romantic restaurants on Maui for introverts.

Hours: 7am-10am for breakfast, 10am-1:45pm for lunch, 6:30pm-9:45pm for dinner ***Meals:*** Breakfast, Lunch, Dinner ***Cost:*** \$27-\$60 ***Known For:*** Japanese, Sushi ***View:*** Gorgeous views from high up on Haleakala overlooking Molokini, Kaho'olawe, and Lana'i. ***Kid-friendly:*** Yes, for sophisticated kids! Limited kid's menu, too. ***Alcohol:*** Yes ***Website:*** www.diamondresort.com ***Reservations:*** Recommended ***Credit Cards:*** All Major

Location: South Maui, Wailea Diamond Hawaii Resort, 555 Kaukahi St. ***808-874-0500*** ***How to Find:*** In the Diamond Hawaii Resort. From Wailea Alanui Drive, turn left on Kaukahi St., just past the Kea Lani Resort. Follow to the end, where you'll find Diamond Hawaii Resort & Spa Hawaii. ***Parking:*** Valet, limited parking in lot immediately to right as you arrive.

Top Dessert
Top Kihei Restaurant
ROY'S

Ambience: 22 ***Food:*** 23
Service: 20 ***Value:*** 21
Overall: 86

At Roy's, every night is a wonderful surprise. Celebrated chef Roy Yamaguchi shapes his menu around the freshest ingredients of that day, often listing up to 25 specials each evening. He also keeps a select few of his "classics" on the menu.

Our favorite classics include the misoyaki butterfish and the roasted macadamia nut mahi mahi with an outrageous lobster butter sauce. We also like the short ribs. Another favorite fish preparation is the wasabi pistachio nut crust with the avocado mousse. It's not always on the menu, but if it is, it's worth a try.

If you're in the mood for beef, they have wonderful tenderloin and other preparations, too. In short, wearing out the menu is practically impossible.

Yamaguchi's vast experience (22 Roy restaurants around the world, including New York, Austin, and San Francisco) informs his menu, which demonstrates the height of Hawaiian Regional Cuisine. As one of the twelve founding members of the revolutionary movement, his food is a heady mix of European sauces and Asian spices applied to seafood and meat.

The service is well-trained, and the servers all know their stuff – you can rely upon them to guide you well.

We often go and order a selection of pupus rather than focusing on the entrées to get the amazing cuisine at a less expensive price.

The wine list is beautiful, and the servers will be happy to recommend something to complement your meal – with such unusual combinations of ingredients, you can easily get lost.

While some find these restaurants noisy, we actually enjoy the joyful bustle of the exhibition kitchen and the often bubbly diners.

The Melting Hot Chocolate Soufflé is a must for dessert. Order it early so it's ready on time. Also very good: the banana crisp. Maybe you should order both.

Hours: Nightly, 5:30pm-10pm (last reservation at 9:15) ***Meals:*** Dinner
Cost: $25-$55 ***Known For:*** Hawaiian Regional Cuisine, Seafood, Steaks
View: None, although lots of local artists on the walls.
Kid-friendly: Yes ***Alcohol:*** Yes, full bar ***Website:*** www.roysrestaurant.com
Reservations: Recommended ***Credit Cards:*** All Major
Location: Pi'ilani Shopping Center, (near Safeway and Outback Steakhouse), 303 Piikea Ave., Kihei ***808-891-1120***

Location: Kahana Gateway Shopping Center, 4405 Hwy. 30, Lahaina ***808-669-6999*** ***Parking:*** Parking Lot

---

Top Burger and Shake
Top Kid-Friendly Restaurant

RUBY'S

Ambience: 18 ***Food:*** 20
Service: 21 ***Value:*** 22
Overall: 81

Ahh, Ruby's. We've seen them in airports and malls across the country, but this location is special. We suspect the franchise owner is on-site continually, because the service, cleanliness, and consistently high-quality food makes this diner a pleasure to eat in.

Located in the mall, this is one of our favorite spots to grab a bite before going to the MACC for Wednesday night films (the Maui Arts & Cultural Center is a beautiful theater modeled on Carnegie Hall, and every Wednesday Barry Rivers and the Maui Film Festival brings a first-run movie to the hall - usually one that can't be seen elsewhere on the island).

We love the thick and juicy burgers, especially the Guacamole Burger and the Mushroom Burger. They are served wrapped in waxed paper to keep the ingredients from spilling out as you take your first bites.

The milkshakes are delicious and thick, and they will make them anyway you please, with an extra shot of dark chocolate, etc. You don't just get what fits in the glass - you also get the metal container with the rest of the goods. And if you ask, they'll split one shake into two, each with their own glass, whipped cream, and cherry on top.

The fries and onion rings are crispy and light.

The fajitas are OK, but we'd go to Fred's for those. However, if you're in the mood for something cheesy and find yourself here, try the buffalo chicken quesadillas. Simple chunks of their very good buffalo chicken strips smothered in cheese and sandwiched between two flour tortillas, these are surprisingly tasty. Served on a nice plate with fresh guacamole, cooling sour cream, and spicy homemade salsa, this is a very satisfying meal.

A very good entrée is the turkey dinner - complete with mashed potatoes, stuffing, gravy, and a tart cranberry sauce - this is a surprisingly good meal. The air conditioning is usually turned up in this restaurant, so it's easy to pretend you're not in the tropics and can afford the heavy food.

Best burger and milkshake on the island, hands down.

Hours: Sunday-Thursday, 7am-9pm; Friday-Saturday 7am-10pm
Meals: Breakfast, Lunch, Dinner ***Cost:*** $7-$20
Known For: Breakfast, Burgers, Ice Cream, Salads, Sandwiches
Kid-friendly: Yes ***Website:*** www.rubys.com
Credit Cards: All Major

Location: Central Maui, Kahului Queen Ka-Kaahumanu Center, 275 W. Kaahumanu ***808-248-7829***
How to Find: Just at the mall entrance - you can't miss it ***Parking:*** Parking lot.

RUTH'S CHRIS STEAK HOUSE

Ambience: 22 ***Food:*** 18
Service: 22 ***Value:*** 17
Overall: 79

We've never been particularly impressed with this expensive chain, and we're definitely not impressed with either the Lahaina or Wailea locations. While the food is certainly not bad, it's not great, either, and we think you can do much better for your money, especially on Maui.

The Lahaina location has a view of the seawall and Lahaina harbor going for it, and the service in both locations is very good. The restaurants are well-staffed, you don't have to wait for bread or water, and they seem to have plenty of time to help you decide what to eat. They also are generally knowledgeable about the menu. The wine list is very nice, and there are several half bottles of excellent wines, which makes it easy to splurge but not overdo it.

We are steak lovers and completely agree with Ruth's Chris stated philosophy on preparation: start with quality meat, season with salt and pepper, broil until done (we like it medium rare), and put it on a hot plate with butter and a little fresh parsley. A good cut of meat doesn't need to be pounded, manipulated, or sauced to death in order to taste wonderful.

So why don't their steaks taste better? We're honestly not sure. They claim USDA Prime on most of their cuts, and we believe them. Has corn-fed beef really lost so much flavor? (After eating Maui Cattle Company beef, grass-fed on the slopes of Haleakala, we think maybe so.)

The T-Bone, which should be a superior cut, never wows us. We're looking for succulence and rich, hearty flavor perhaps spiced with a dash of earthy-tasting iron, but we get. . .not even close to that. The filet tastes better, but it's so soft in texture that we wonder if it wasn't marinated in a tenderizer (a crime for the kind of cut they claim to serve).

The creamed spinach is quite good. The spinach chopped so fine it creates almost a silky butter, and we would choose it over the chunkier version we usually prefer. Meanwhile, though, the potatoes au gratin are too chunky. The whole point of the dish is to slice the potatoes so thin that as they cook they become nearly indiscernible from the layers of cheese between. Here, they are cut into chunks and mixed with cheese that looks like the cheddar you use for Kraft macaroni dinners (no, we don't think it's a mix, just a bad choice of cheese). The result, instead of being a pleasant melding of sweet root vegetable and smooth dairy, is tangy cheesy strings wrapped around mealy potatoes.

The desserts are all brought in from the mainland, and they're fine for what they are. There is a severe shortage of good pastry chefs on island, so we always cut a lot of slack on dessert menus.

But what are you doing ordering dessert, anyway? We say skip the dessert, skip the sides, skip the meat, and skip the appetizers. If you're hungry for steak there are better choices on island: if you're in South Maui, go to Longhi's or Joe's; if you're on the north shore or upcountry, go to Makawao Steak House; and if you're in West Maui, go to Maui Brewing Company, Longhi's or Pineapple Grill.

Hours: Daily 5-9pm ***Meals:*** Dinner ***Cost:*** $23-50
Known For: Steak ***Alcohol:*** Full bar
Website: www.ruthschris.com ***Credit Cards:*** All Major

Location: South Maui, Wailea 3750 Wailea Alanui Dr. ***808-874-8880***
How to Find: in the Shops at Wailea ***Parking:*** free parking available

Location: West Maui, Lahaina 900 Front St. ***808-661-8815***
How to Find: Across from the sea wall on Front St.
Parking: Street, parking lots.

Top Vietnamese
Top Restaurant in Wailuku
A SAIGON CAFÉ

Ambience: 16 *Food:* 20
Service: 20 *Value:* 21
Overall: 77

Despite a terrible location and just barely acceptable ambience, this is one of our favorite restaurants. Moderate prices, great fresh food, and a staff full of attentive, funny, quick servers make it a great experience.

Start with the lemonade – with a splash of lime juice it's worth the $2.50.

The "fondue" is wonderful. You get rice paper, a plate full of veggies, sprouts, pickled cabbage and carrots, and raw fish, meat, pork, or chicken. Then they put a fondue pot on the table, full of simmering stew with vegetables and pineapple. You cook your own meat in the fondue, and then assemble your rolls.

It's fun, festive, and delicious.

The servers will hang around until you demonstrate that you can handle the rice paper and assemble the ingredients properly – and if you fumble, they'll step in and make things right. It's a blast.

Meanwhile, the noodle dishes and pho are uniformly excellent.

Researching this guide can be tough – we have to eat a lot of food that isn't good, and we both can get rather cranky when we've been paying top dollar for so-so food. When that happens, we comfort ourselves at A Saigon Café with the fresh fish platter. A full fish (yes, head and tail included) is served steamed or deep-fried (we like both preparations) and plated over crispy steamed vegetables in a delicious soy-based sauce. Rice is served on the side. As we pluck delicious morsels from between the ribs, our bodies relax and we start to remember all the good food that is available on Maui.

The bar has a nice selection of beer and wine, and in general, this little hideaway is a gem waiting for tourists to discover it. Although it can be difficult to find, it's worth the extra effort.

The waiters will make a lot of jokes - be prepared - and there's no way to stop them. Just call it the floor show and enjoy yourself.

Hours: Monday-Saturday, 10am-9:30pm; Sunday 10am-8:30pm
Meals: Lunch, Dinner ***Cost:*** $9-35 ***Known For:*** Vietnamese
Kid-friendly: Yes ***Alcohol:*** Yes, full bar.
Reservations: Recommended.
Credit Cards: DS, M, VS

Location: Central Maui, Wailuku 1792 Main St. ***808-243-9560***
How to Find: This is "under" the highway overpass in Wailuku. Look for the neon lit shooting stars and the pink building to the right of the highway overpass as you drive into Wailuku on Ka'ahumanu Ave. Turn right at the light, then take your first right, drive to the first stop sign, and turn right. Restaurant is on the left, 1 block. It's worth it! ***Parking:*** Parking lot. Street.

Top Late Night Dining

SANSEI SEAFOOD RESTAURANT & SUSHI BAR

Ambience: 20 *Food:* 20
Service: 18 *Value:* 21
Overall: 79

For locals, the Kihei Sansei is the Maui equivalent of the TV classic "Cheers!," minus the snarky waitress.

Everyone knows your name, because just about everyone shows up half an hour before they open on Sunday or Monday to take advantage of the half-price specials from 5 to 6pm. We all stand in line, anxiously waiting to hear if we have a table, a place at the sushi bar, or a place at the cocktail bar.

The food is worth the effort, especially at these prices. Sansei's menu features inventive and dynamic Pacific Rim-influenced Japanese dishes. There are very good traditional teriyaki chicken and beef dishes, along with plenty of fresh fish preparations - and then there's the sushi. You can get standards here, as well as many veggie rolls.

The over-the-top rolls are also fun to try, and they're what Sansei does best. The Caterpillar, which is an eel roll, is layered with ahi and salmon. There is also a very good miso butterfish dish as an appetizer. The spicy crab rolls, panko-crusted ahi sashimi, and Asian rock-shrimp cakes are all delicious.

The tempura is very good - and speaking of tempura, you must try the tempura-fried ice cream with chocolate sauce.

If you sit at the bar, you're in for a treat. You can order from the full menu, and the bartenders know how to put on a show. Tell them what kind of tastes you want in your drink, and they'll invent something on the spot for you and present it with a flourish.

The Kapalua location has the same 50% off deal on Sundays and Mondays from 5 to 6pm. Both locations feature 25% savings from 5:30 to 6pm every night, and every night after 10pm all sushi bar items are 50% off (both locations). While you're indulging in late night sushi, put your name in for Karaoke.

Meals: Dinner *Cost:* $15-$45 (sushi can be a lot or a little, depending on how you order) *Known For:* Japanese, Pacific Rim, Seafood, Sushi
Kid-friendly: Yes *Alcohol:* Yes, full bar *Reservations:* Recommended
Website: www.dkrestaurants.com *Credit Cards:* All Major

Location: West Maui, Kapalua 600 Office Rd. ***808-669-6286***
How to Find: In Kapalua Resort.
Hours: Daily 5:30-10pm; Thursday-Friday 5:30pm-1am

Location: South Maui, Kihei 1881 S. Kihei Rd. ***808-879-0004***
How to Find: Kihei Town Center near Foodland (S. Kihei Rd.), Kihei
Hours: Nightly, 5:30-10pm; Thursday-Saturday 10pm-1am for Late Night Specials

---

SARENTO'S ON THE BEACH

Ambience: 23 *Food:* 18
Service: 18 *Value:* 17
Overall: 76

The last time we went to Sarento's - and we would make it our last time if we didn't have a responsibility to you to go back and keep this review "fresh" - we had a wonderfully ironic experience that explicitly illustrates our feelings about this beautiful-but-deeply-flawed restaurant.

We were seated with another couple, also locals, at a prime table by the wide open windows. The waves were crashing on the beach not 30 feet away, the sun was setting, and we all felt beautiful and content. Our wine had arrived (after much tussling amongst ourselves over which overpriced bottle to buy from their much-celebrated wine list) and we were relaxing and enjoying the breeze while contemplating the dinner menu.

A woman's voice broke in to our peaceful companionship and chirped "Would you like a photo of yourselves to take home with you? You can pick up four prints on the way out this evening, and they're only $20 a piece!"

We all turned, menus still up, and stared at her blankly. She was holding a large camera rig with a big flash system, dressed in black and white, with comfortable shoes, as if she were shooting a wedding. Jim waited a beat, and then said "We're kama'aina (locals)."

She immediately grew a little pale, tootled "Oops! Sorry!" and scuttled off to a table at the other end of the dining room. We all continued to stare after her, completely unable to believe what had just happened.

Is this Disneyland? Sometimes we wonder.

Sarento's is one of the tourist traps we review solely so you can avoid it. Yes, *Wine Spectator* gives it an award every year for their magnificent wine list. Yes, it is almost perilously close to the ocean, on one of the most beautiful beaches on the island (Keawakapu, pronounced "Kay-ah-vah-kah-poo"). Yes, it has outstanding sunsets. Yes, some of their dishes (especially those with lobster and other shellfish) are very good. Yes, the servers dress formally, and the hostess always looks overwhelmingly adorable, with hair hanging just below her pencil thin waist.

But everything - and we mean everything - is overpriced for the quality (including the wine list, as we alluded to earlier). There is nothing here - save filet mignon meatballs - that you can't get anywhere else on island.

(You don't want these meatballs anyway - using this super tender cut in a dish that requires a lot of fat to make a tasty meatball was a bad idea in the first place. They are dry, flavorless, and usually left on the plate in big crumbles. We believe the reason they are on the menu is so that they can charge $30 for a plate of spaghetti with a "fancy" meat garnish.)

The service is notorious for being both overbearingly boastful and preternaturally slow. As we enter the beautiful reception area and follow the hostess through the slick bar, past the wine cellar and private dining area, into the spacious dining room opening up to the ocean view, we often get the feeling that we are being lured farther and farther into the center of a spider's web. The sticky trap is revealed in the final bill, which is always at least 40% above what we want to or would expect to pay for the same meal elsewhere.

The web analogy, while admittedly rather melodramatic, is the most accurate we can come up with. Sarento's looks gorgeous and unique, tempting you with "you can't find this anywhere else" vibes. But in the end you can - elsewhere on island and possibly in your own hometown - and you pay through the nose for the pleasure of having spent a few (plus) hours being shoved about by high prices, pushy photographers, and sometimes downright snotty waiters.

If you love Italian food and want authentic food in a beautiful setting, head up the hill to the Diamond Hawaii Resort and go to Capische?

Hours: Dinner daily 5:30-10pm, Lounge 5pm-12am ***Meals:*** Dinner
Cost: $28-50 ***Known For:*** Italian ***Kid-Friendly:*** Yes, children's menu
View: Yes, overlooks Molokini, Lanai, and Kaho'olawe
Alcohol: Yes, with an extensive wine list
Website: www.tristarrestaurants.com
Credit Cards: All Major

Location: South Maui, Kihei 2980 S. Kihei Rd. ***808-875-7555***
How to Find: Just past the Kihei Boat Ramp ***Parking:*** Valet

Fr

Top Maui I

Top Breakfas

SEAWATCH

Ambience: 23 *Food:* 22
Service: 19 *Value:* 21
Overall: 85

On Maui, you can easily drop $30 per person on a buffet breakfast at the resorts. But you don't have to.

If you're in South Maui, there's a steal of a deal right up the slopes of Halealakala, where the Wailea Golf Course features the lovely SeaWatch Restaurant.

Overlooking the lower golf course and stunning views of Molokini, Kaho'olawe, and breaching whales in season, this restaurant can't be beat for views. You can eat inside or out (who wants to eat inside, anyway, with views like this?), and the service is uniformly friendly and prompt.

It's one of South Maui's best restaurants for overall value.

If you go for sunset, you've made a good choice. The lava flows are particularly good for cocktails, and the chilled tiger prawns over blue crab salad are the perfect way to celebrate this view.

The rack of lamb is delicious and tender, and the tataki-style ahi with sesame Alaskan scallops in a wasabi butter sauce is a favorite.

The fresh fish preparations are all delectable, so ask for a thorough description of the day's specials. If available, we especially like the Citrus preparation with the sweet and spicy flavors of sweet tea, lemongrass, and coconut rice.

Lunch is also a great value – the sandwiches, pastas, salads, and wraps are well-priced and all well worth it. The kalua pig sandwich is one of the best on the island.

But we have to admit; we usually eat lunch and dinner at other restaurants and go to SeaWatch for breakfast. Every day is Sunday Brunch here with breakfast and lunch served from morning through afternoon.

and at $10 for the best eggs benedict we've ever eaten (the Hollandaise remarkable), it beats out breakfast standards like the Kihei Caffe for price.

If you're going to spend $10 on breakfast, why not get 10-million-dollar-views? Much like their sister restaurant the Plantation House in Kapalua, this place gets our vote for best overall value: great food at truly reasonable prices, and beautiful views with attentive service.

Hours: Daily 8am-10pm ***Meals:*** Breakfast, Lunch, Dinner ***Cost:*** $13-$35
Known For: Breakfast, Burgers, Sandwiches, Seafood
View: Spectacular sunset dining, gorgeous views from on high of Molokini, Kaho'olawe, and Lana'i. ***Kid-friendly:*** Yes. ***Alcohol:*** Yes, full bar.
Website: www.seawatch.com ***Reservations:*** Recommended at night.
Credit Cards: All Major

Location: South Maui, Wailea 100 Wailea Golf Club Drive ***808-875-8080***
How to Find: Turn up into the Wailea Golf Club's second entrance from Wailea Alanui. ***Parking:*** Parking lot, valet.

SHAKA

Ambience: 16 ***Food:*** 18
Service: 17 ***Value:*** 15
Overall: 66

Shaka is an East Coast-style pizzeria, and it wins lots of local awards. That might be because few on Maui knows how pizza is supposed to really taste – and there's not much competition out here.

Fresh ingredients, gourmet toppings, and thin crust (they also make a "Sicilian") all make this pizza look great – but for our East Coast palette, it's still not "real" pizza. The crust is okay, but the tomato sauce is lacking a complexity we need in really good pizza, where the sauce is the star of the show.

You'll do better with the white pizza – cheese, olive oil, garlic, and gourmet toppings like clam and spinach. Still, we'd order a slice before ordering a whole pizza.

Luckily, they have really good hot sandwiches. Try the sausage or meatball sandwich. And if Philly cheese steaks are your thing, you'll be pretty satisfied at Shaka's. The prices are high, but you can split them with your buddy and get a good value.

Hours: Daily 10:30am-9pm, 'til 10pm on Friday and Saturday
Meals: Lunch, Dinner ***Cost:*** $8-$20 ***Known For:*** Pizza, Sandwiches
Kid-friendly: Yes ***Credit Cards:*** MC, VS

Location: South Maui, Kihei 1770 S. Kihei Rd. ***808-874-0331***
How to Find: Across from the Kukui Mall. ***Parking:*** Parking lot

---

SON'Z

Ambience: 21 ***Food:*** 17
Service: 17 ***Value:*** 15
Overall: 70

To get to Son'z in the Ka'anapali Hyatt Regency you walk through the shopping mall and descend a sweeping staircase. A spacious bar and a large, warmly decorated dining room are sheltered from the wind and open on to one of the most romantic views in Maui: a waterfall-fed pond dotted with elegant white swans. Protected by the pond from the beach-walk-gawkers and by the waterfalls from other restaurants, this is a beautiful spot for an intimate evening.

Unfortunately, the location cannot make up for the over-priced, so-so food. Our first reaction when looking at the menu is always confusion. The font is a cheery handwritten style that doesn't match the overwrought descriptions and significant dollar amounts. The menu at Nick's, their sister restaurant, shares the font and many of the same dishes seem to rotate between the two establishments. The preparations all sound unusual, but also unappetizing, and that is too often what they turn out to be.

Turning to the staff for help in ordering is rarely helpful. The answer tends to be "whatever you like" and an even more elaborate description of the many ingredients, rather than a carefully considered opinion based on their personal preferences.

When pressed on a recent visit, the server said that the following items were "popular," but when we probed he wouldn't equate that to "very good," just repeated "these are our most popular dishes."

One of those "popular" selections is the Hawaiian opakapaka picatta. We were not sure we should order it, because it sounded too much, and it was. Artichokes, caperberries (a berry with a milder-than-caper flavor) and lemon are sautéed with the pink snapper, which is piled on top of a sweet potato hash brown. A dark red tomato puree is poured around the dish. The presentation is strikingly unappealing. One of the problems is a garish use of color – every one in the rainbow is on the plate, including purple in the hash browns. The sweet potatoes are purple because they are from Molokai – but since they aren't listed that way on the menu, the deep color is a surprise. Once tasted, however, the normally sweet and hefty potatoes taste like . . . nothing. Absolutely no flavor. That actually turns out to be a blessing, since all the other flavors simply don't work well together.

Another "popular" dish, and a more successful one in some ways, is the veal. Sometimes the menu lists a pan-roasted cotelette – or cutlet – and sometimes it lists a chop. It's always served with a delicious rosemary späetzle, a German noodle dish, but you have to scrape off most of the maitake-porcini mustard sauce to keep it from ruining your enjoyment of the späetzle. This is an excellent example of a typical comment we make about this restaurateur – overly ambitious dishes that end up not working because there is just one too many elements. Although we love the spaetzle, we've had soggy veal cutlets and more-than-done chops.

We do like the rhubarb pie for dessert, and we also like their mai tais (the lava flows taste like they're from a mix, though). They have an impressive wine list and claim a 3,000 bottle wine cellar, the largest around with a value reported to be over $250,000.

Something about the sometimes stilted service - it sounds like they're speaking from an executive-mandated script, and they often hold their hands in the stereotypical waiter's pose, elbows akimbo, left hand facing up with right hand placed on top and facing down, fingers stiffened - makes us feel like they're being watched and judged and are afraid of a misstep. The food tastes that way, too, and for these prices there should be a lot more love cooked in. If the kitchen feels the way the servers seem to, we're not sure anyone could expect them to be relaxed and focused enough to turn out a great meal. We hope that this is almost-new restaurant jitters.

If you are staying in Ka'anapali and want to eat a romantic dinner without driving into Lahaina or out to Kapalua, we recommend heading upstairs to the Cascades Grille & Sushi Bar or if you don't mind watching people walk by on the beach walk, Tropica at the Westin.

Hours: Daily 5:30-10pm ***Meals:*** Dinner ***Cost:*** $40 and up
Known For: Pasta, Seafood, Steak ***Kid-Friendly:*** Yes, kid's menu.
View: Romantic water garden setting with the ocean beyond.
Alcohol: Yes, full bar ***Website:*** www.sonzmaui.com
Reservations: Recommended ***Credit Cards:*** All Major

Location: West Maui, Ka'anapali 200 Nohea Kai Dr. ***808-667-4506***
How to Find: in the Hyatt Regency ***Parking:*** Valet

Top Fine Dining

SPAGO

Ambience: 24 ***Food:*** 24
Service: 22 ***Value:*** 20
Overall: 90

This is one of the most beautiful restaurants on Maui. The views are breathtaking in the open-air restaurant, and the exquisite Four Seasons Resort provides a perfect setting for any special occasion.

This location is one of the newest of Wolfgang Puck's celebrated restaurants, and it's worth his name. Fresh local produce, fish, and meats are featured in every dish, and you'll have some heavy decisionmaking to do when you look at the menu.

For appetizers, we especially like the spice ahi poke in little sesame "cones." When you bite the crisp cone and the ahi starts melting on your tongue, it heralds a great meal.

The Kula greens with goat cheese and onions is a delicious salad with tangy balsamic vinaigrette.

The menu changes depending upon what's available that day, but most preparations remain consistent. For instance, the Shrimp and Opakapaka preparation with pineapple curry and jasmine rice is out of this world. And if you're in the mood for a steak, we highly recommend the tender and juicy tenderloin.

If you want to eat like Hawaiian Ali'i (royalty), get the wok-fried fish (especially if it's moi, a tender white fish reserved only for kings in the old days). The spectacular presentation of a deep-fried fish on a bed of Thai veggies is incredible. After it arrives, the waiter will filet it for you so that you don't have to deal with the head and tail if you don't want tor.

There's a lovely wine list, and the drinks are potent and creative. The service is white-glove European, yet authentically Aloha.

The lounge outside this restaurant is our favorite place to head after work. Gorgeous sunset views combined with delicious cocktails and the best people-watching on Maui (we won't tell you who, but let's just say that lots of celebrities have been spotted here) make it a must-do.

This is one of our very favorite special occasion restaurants.

Hours: Nightly, 5:30pm-9:30pm ***Meals:*** Dinner ***Cost:*** $38-120
Known For: Pacific Rim, Seafood, Steak ***View:*** Gorgeous of the resort, West Maui Mountains, Molokini, Kaho'olawe, and Lana'i.
Kid-friendly: Yes ***Alcohol:*** Yes, full bar ***Website:*** www.fourseasons.com
Reservations: Required ***Credit Cards:*** All

Location: South Maui, Wailea ***808-879-2999***
The Four Seasons Resort, 3900 Wailea Alanui Dr
Parking: Valet

STELLA BLUES

Ambience: 19 ***Food:*** 19
Service: 19 ***Value:*** 18
Overall: 75

Stella Blues is like a pair of old slippers – well worn, but so comfortable, you keep putting them on, hoping they'll last just one more year. We hope Stella, which has been open since 1994, lasts much longer. Their American comfort food with a Southern twist, exhibition kitchen, outdoor seating, and pool tables make them a local favorite.

The menu features everything from tofu to short ribs, and every plate is piled high with tasty food made from high quality local ingredients. One of our favorites is the baby back ribs slow-roasted, then grilled and brushed with a fruity tropical barbecue sauce. Served with cornbread (hearty, yellow, Southern style cornbread) and slaw, this is a very satisfying meal.

We also like the "All American Meal" with half a roasted chicken, mashed potatoes (rich and smooth), creamed corn, and wilted spinach. The tofu entrees (yes, there are more than one) include curries and stir fries.

Skip the coconut shrimp – a tricky dish to master – as we too often find it overdone and less fresh than we'd like. However, the Maui Cattle Company short ribs and steaks are wonderful, as is the thick and rich meatloaf.

This is not fine cuisine, but it is true food, prepared by people who care about what they're doing. The décor is open, blond, and sturdy, and you can sit outside in the fenced in tiki-torched lanai (this is in a strip mall, so a fence shields you from the parking lot) or inside in chilly-for-Maui air conditioning. Or sit at the bar or eat on the edge of the pool table. The service is good, and this is a great place to hang out.

Hours: Breakfast Monday-Saturday 7:30-11am, Sun. 7:30am-2pm; Lunch 11am-4pm; Dinner 5-10pm ***Meals:*** Breakfast, Lunch, Dinner
Cost: $15-31 ***Known For:*** Breakfast, Burgers, Sandwiches, Seafood, Steak
Kid-Friendly: Yes ***Alcohol:*** Yes, full bar
Website: www.stellablues.com
Credit Cards: All Major

Location: South Maui, Kihei 1279 S. Kihei Rd. ***808-874-3779***
How to Find: Azeka Mauka Shopping Center
Parking: shopping center parking lot.

TASAKA GURI-GURI

We insist that you stop in at Tasaka's for a cup of their delicious Guri-Guri. It will take you no time at all, and you will not find this something-like-ice-cream-but-also-like-sherbet treat anywhere else (even other places on Oahu aren't the same).

Two melon-ball sized scoops in a Dixie cup cost you a whole $1, and you can choose from the two available flavors.

The Tasaka family closely guards the recipe, although when pressed they'll admit that you can get all the ingredients at any grocery store . . . except for one mystery ingredient. The Food Network loves this place, and so does Bill Clinton. The third generation is running the business now, and we're a little worried that they'll get bored, close up shop, and take the recipe with them . . . so hurry hurry and get your Guri-Guri.

Hours: Daily 9am-6pm ***Cost:*** $1
Known For: Japanese Ice Cream ***Kid-Friendly:*** Yes

Location: Central Maui, Kahului 70 E Kaahumanu Ave ***808-871-4513***
How to Find: In the Maui Mall near the pet store.
Parking: Mall parking lot.

TASTY CRUST

Ambience: 5 ***Food:*** 15
Service: 15 ***Value:*** 15
Overall: 50

Tasty Crust features local style food, and lots of it, at rock-bottom prices in a restaurant that hasn't been updated (or cleaned?) in decades. This is a "landmark" local diner on Maui, and while that could promise charm and nostalgia, it has neither.

A lot depends upon your server. You're either going to get sweet, or salty. . .and salty combined with dingy paneled walls, cafeteria booths, and sticky tables doesn't cut it. Especially when the "world famous" hotcakes taste just like the baking soda that makes them so fluffy.

That said, the prices are truly cheap, for Maui or anywhere else, and it can be fun to eat in a dive of a greasy spoon and compare it to your local dive of a greasy spoon. Kids like it – everything's on the menu, and it's noisy and smells of grease and sugar.

Hours: Monday 6am-3pm; Tuesday-Thursday and Sunday 6am-10pm; Friday-Saturday 6am-11pm ***Meals:*** Breakfast, Lunch, Dinner
Cost: $8 and under ***Known For:*** Breakfast, Local, Sandwiches
Kid-Friendly: Yes No Credit Cards, but Debit Cards accepted

Location: Central Maui, Wailuku 1770 Mill St. ***808-244-0845***
How to Find: From Kahului Beach Rd. bear left on Lower Main St. Bear right on Mill St. ***Parking:*** Lot

Top Thai
THAILAND CUISINE

Ambience: 20 *Food:* 22
Service: 20 *Value:* 22
Overall: 84

This is one of our favorite restaurants on Maui. It's not fancy (although the statues and paintings are all very beautiful) and it's located in shopping malls, but the food is uniformly delicious, the service is very good, and the prices are moderate.

Fresh island produce, homegrown herbs, and imported ingredients make one of the best versions of this complex, heady cuisine we've had.

It's as good as any Thai in big cities, and we eat here at least two times a month. All dishes can be made to any degree of "heat" (spice) you like - but if you want authentic Thai, order "Thai Hot," which is hotter than "Hot."

We always order the tom ka gai, the spicy coconut soup with chicken and shrimp. We like it Thai hot with sticky rice stirred in to cut the spice a tad. This soup is consistently the most comforting blend of sweet and stimulating spice we know, and it always preps us well for the next course.

Everything is served family style and most dishes serve two to three. We like the sweet and spicy Thai Beefsteak served over a bed of greens. We also like the spicy pork larb and the delicious green papaya salad.

Other standouts are the Evil Prince curry with tofu (there's a large selection of vegetable and tofu entrees, by the way) and the red curry.

The beer and wine list is limited in scope, but all we really want is Singha when we eat Thai, and that is always available.

Thai menus are extensive, and this one has everything you can imagine included. Make sure you get the tapioca pudding for dessert. Made with coconut milk, even lactose intolerant types melt over its creamy goodness.

Hours: Daily, Dinner 5pm-10pm, Monday-Saturday, Lunch 11am-2:30pm
Meals: Lunch, Dinner ***Cost:*** $9-$15 ***Known For:*** Thai
Kid-friendly: Yes ***Alcohol:*** Yes, wine and beer
Website: www.thailandcuisinemaui.com ***Credit Cards:*** All Major

Location: Central Maui, Kahului 70 E. Kaahumanu Ave. ***808-873-0225***
How to Find: Maui Mall Shopping Center

Location: South Maui, Kihei 1819 S. Kihei Rd. ***808-875-0839***
How to Find: Kukui Mall, near Starbucks

TOMMY BAHAMA'S TROPICAL CAFÉ

Ambience: 22 ***Food:*** 19
Service: 18 ***Value:*** 18
Overall: 77

Tommy Bahama, maker of island-inspired apparel (which you can buy in the "emporium" attached to the restaurant), has a pricy-but-decent café in the Shops at Wailea.

The casual cuisine and great bar make for a good meal, although we tend to visit Longhi's first for value.

Good dishes include incredible crab cakes. The coconut shrimp are also very yummy and crunchy. The Habana Cabana pork sandwich – pulled pork with blackberry brandy barbeque sauce – is one of our very favorite items. The pork is tender and squelches with the sweet sauce.

We also like the cheeseburger, made with Black Angus meat, cheddar, hickory bacon and – our favorite – honey roasted onions.

The salads are fresh and make a wonderful and satisfying meal on their own. We especially like the chopped salad with chicken, granny smith apples, macadamia nuts, bacon, and sweet corn.

Other favorites include jerk chicken or pork, curried shrimp and sea scallops, pork chops, a nice bass preparation, and the tenderloin. The ribs in the blackberry brandy sauce are also good.

Desserts are very good at Tommy's (we often go to Longhi's for dinner, then head up here if we're still aching for something sweet). Try the Pina Colada cake, the bread pudding, or the key lime pie. And the brownie sundae is tremendous.

If you're at the Shops and need a good meal but Cheeseburger in Paradise is too downmarket and Longhi's is too upscale, this is a decent choice, though many feel it's just too overpriced, especially at dinner.

Hours: Daily, 11am-10pm ***Meals:*** Lunch, Dinner ***Cost:*** $18-$35
Known For: Burgers, Salads, Sandwiches, Steak
View: Condos built in 2004. ***Kid-friendly:*** Yes
Alcohol: Yes, full bar ***Website:*** www.tommybahama.com
Reservations: Recommended ***Credit Cards:*** All Major

Location: South Maui, Wailea 3750 Wailea Alanui Drive ***808-875-9983***
How to Find: In the Shops at Wailea ***Parking:*** Parking Lot

---

Top Ka'anapali Restaurant
TROPICA

Ambience: 22 ***Food:*** 22
Service: 20 ***Value:*** 22
Overall: 86

Sometimes a hotel restaurant does food right, and Tropica is one of them. One of the best things about this restaurant is the wide-ranging menu. A large appetizer menu, lots of salads, excellent pizzas, and a whole range of shish kebabs make a lighter and less expensive dinner not only possible but varied and flavorful. A big dessert menu makes late-night snackers happy and the excellent selection of entrees makes a soup-to-nuts meal inevitable. Wine suggestions are listed with every item.

Although the appetizer portions are small, we think that sharing a few and adding a salad or pizza make a nice meal. Try the excellent ahi roll with a panko crust. Served on a bed of salad greens with pohole ferns and seaweed, the presentation is perfect. The sear on the ahi is perfect, and the fish itself is fresh. This roll has out-Sansei'ed Sansei for presentation.

We also love the scallops wrapped with bacon. Although this traditional combination can be heavy and rich, the corn cake served alongside provides the perfect salty crumble to go with the sweet and rich fish. The scallop is very tender and the bacon perfectly crisp and it is an intensely flavorful dish.

The seafood paella is one of our favorite dishes. The lobster claw is placed to hide the tail underneath while clams, mussels, scallops, fish, and mussels swim underneath in lovely saffron rice. The deliciously aromatic broth is garlicky and very good. It's obvious to us that the chef is putting a lot of thought and care into his dishes.

If you're in the mood for chicken, this is one of our favorite places to get it. A half-roasted chicken arrives with crisp flavorful asparagus and sweet roasted carrots. Whipped potatoes are piled high, and this comforting meal may be just the antidote to an overload of tropical fish and rum drinks.

One of our favorite desserts on Maui is served at Tropica. It may sound a little childlike, but their ice cream sandwiches are really, really good, and very adult. Ginger snap cookies made in the hotel bakery - and deliciously intense - are layered with ice cream and laced with caramel. While we like the crème brulee just fine, and the chocolate macadamia cheesecake mousse is good too, the ice cream sandwich is our favorite.

If you pick your eyes off your plate, you'll see an amazing view of Ka'anapali beach and the ocean, although you will also see beach-goers walking by on the beach walk. The décor seems a little schizophrenic: giant thatched umbrellas over heavy wooden tables and chairs arranged around a glossy koi pond fed by waterfalls at the front of the restaurant, with an upscale, modern wall-of-water fountain on a searing blue wall behind a large glass bar and a gleaming exhibition kitchen at the back. It's all a little less than elegant at first glance, and screams Hawaiian-tourist-trap. Luckily, it isn't.

Live music at night - usually a laid back Hawaiian guy crooning love songs with his guitar his only companion - and flickering tiki torches lining the beach walk directly in front of the *al fresco* dining make this a fairly romantic setting at night. And a single taste of the delicious key lime martini could more than open you up for what the night has to offer.

This is an excellent choice if you are staying in Ka'anapali and don't want to drive anywhere for dinner.

Hours: Daily 3-9:30pm ***Meals:*** Happy Hour, Dinner
Cost: $15-45 ***Known For:*** Seafood, Steak
Kid-Friendly: Yes ***View:*** Pacific Ocean and neighboring islands
Alcohol: Yes, full bar ***Website:*** www.westinmaui.com
Reservations recommended ***Credit Cards:*** All Major

Location: West Maui, Lahaina 2365 Ka'anapali Pkwy ***808-667-2525***
How to Find: Right on the beach in the Westin Maui
Parking: Valet or park at Whaler's Village and walk over.

TUTU'S

If you want to protect yourself from criticism in Hawaii, be the only game in town and call yourself Tutu (grandmother). It's hard to complain about someone's little grandma, right? Especially when she's feeding you in Hana, the most beautiful place on earth and what even Hawaiians call "the most Hawaiian of places."

Most people who mention Tutu's say "it's the only place to eat lunch in Hana." That is true. If you go to the Hana Ranch you'll be ripped off by the prices and leave hungry because the food is barely edible. If you go to the Hana Hotel, you will pay a lot for very good food . . . but since they're the only place to eat dinner in town, you're probably already eating there that evening.

If you go to Tutu's for lunch, you may feel relieved that you can digest your meal that costs less than $8. As for the food . . . it's edible, and it's on the beach, and we really can't say more than that. If you've just driven from Pa'ia or Lahaina, and didn't take our advice to bring a lunch with you . . . you will have to be satisfied with what you find at Tutu's.

The taro burger is probably the most interesting thing on the menu. Taro is the starchy staple of Hawaiian cuisine, and you might as well try it mixed up with rice, dark purple sweet potato from Molokai, carrots, seeds, and other stuff. Grilled as a veggie burger, it's moist and riotous with color, but we don't particularly like the flavors (too sweet in some bites, too garlicky in others).

Cost: Under $7 ***Known For:*** Burgers, Local ***Kid-Friendly:*** Yes
View: Gorgeous black beach and Hana coast

Location: East Maui, Hana 174 Keawe Rd. ***808-248-8224***
How to Find: in Hana Bay right on the beach ***Parking:*** parking lot

---

UPCOUNTRY FRESH TAMALES & MIXED PLATE LOCAL FOOD

Ambience: 17 ***Food:*** 18
Service: 17 ***Value:*** 20
Overall: 72

Upcountry Fresh Tamales lives up to its name as a great place for a quick and cheap meal.

The owner can often be found among fresh Kula corn, using the husks in her out-of-this-world tamales. Daily specials are chipotle pork or chicken mole and are not to be missed.

The service is efficient and they really speak Spanish behind the counter. It's authentic and the prices are reasonable.

Maui's Fresh Tamales recently moved from Makawao Ave., bought the Aloha Mixed Plate, and are now happily serving both local food and tamales. Same quality of food, same cooks ... better location.

Hours: Monday to Saturday, 6am-7:30pm, Sunday 6am-2pm
Meals: Lunch, early dinner ***Cost:*** $7-$9
Known For: Local, Mexican ***Kid-friendly:*** Yes

Location: Upcountry, Pukalani 55 Pukalani Terrace Center, Pukalani
808-572-8258 ***How to Find:*** Next to Foodland. ***Parking:*** Parking Lot

WHO CUT THE CHEESE

Ambience: 18 ***Food:*** 20
Service: 21 ***Value:*** 20
Overall: 79

Who Cut the Cheese is a tiny sparkling gem of a cheese shop in the European tradition, and there's nothing like it anywhere else on Maui.

The sense of humor evident in the name undercuts the seriousness of their enterprise. Meanwhile, the rustic décor and cutesy logo of a mouse with a purple beret might seem foreign to these shores at first, but once you get a taste of the super-competent, knowledgeable, laid-back and friendly service you'll recognize the Aloha that's oozing out of this store.

In short, the ladies who work here know what they're doing. They sell dozens of varieties of both foreign and domestic cheese plus a careful selection of wine, local delicacies, and cured meats. They'll do gift baskets, picnics, and even make you a "jetsetter" packed lunch for your plane ride home.

Free samples are laid out of their recent favorites, and you can spend as long as you like choosing. They'll cut you just a little, or a lot, and if you want one of our very favorite Kihei lunches, ask for a Panini.

You choose your sliced meat or vegetable from their current list, then pair it with your favorite cheese. It takes a few minutes for them to take your selections and grill them between two halves of a La Brea Bread Company par-baked baguette, but it's worth it. While you wait, you can sample some fermented walnuts, sniff some local lavender butter, or do a little wine shopping. There are books and assorted gift items to browse, too.

The sandwiches are divine, and come with a to-go dish of Greek olives and either bottled water or green tea for $10.

The prices on wine are not what you'll pay just next door at Long's (the cheapest place to buy beer, wine, and liquor on island other than Costco), but we don't go into sticker shock here, either. They sell lots of half bottles for beach picnics, which is nice, and their excellent advice and foodie enthusiasm is truly priceless.

One Sunday per month the owner hosts a well-attended (up to fifty) five-course cheese and wine tasting which is definitely worth going to. Call them for details and reserve a ticket for one of the best events to meet local Maui foodies.

Hours: Daily 10am - 7pm ***Meals:*** Panini anytime, snacks wine ***Cost:*** $10
Known For: Cheese, Sandwiches, Wine ***Kid-Friendly:*** Yes ***Alcohol:*** Yes, wine
Website: www.whocutthecheese.net ***Credit Cards:*** All Major

Location: South Maui, Kihei 1279 S. Kihei Rd. ***808-874-3930***
How to Find: In Azeka II Mauka at the corner of Lipoa.
Parking: Mall parking lot.

A Special Invitation to Our Readers . . .

As you'll see in the Introduction, ***Top Maui Restaurants 2008*** is truly a labor of love. Molly and I have recorded a special telephone message for you, our cherished reader.

Please call, toll-free, **1-800-675-3290**, **extension 8**, to listen to a short message available 24-hours a day. The call is free from any phone in the fifty states.

Warm Aloha,
James Jacobson
Kihei, Maui, Hawaii

Get the Latest Updates to Top Maui Restaurants 2008

The Maui restaurant scene changes overnight, which is why our original online version of ***Top Maui Restaurants*** is updated every month of the year. The book you're holding in your hands is accurate as of publication time, but changes are inevitable.

We have built an online community designed for people who are planning their trip to Maui called **www.TopMauiTips.com**. Every member gets a free copy of the current month's ***Top Maui Restaurants*** (a $19.95 value) included in their membership.

We would like to invite you to get the latest copy of the online guide - with more restaurants and fresher reviews - as our free gift to you for buying this book.

To accept our special invitation just for readers of this book, follow these steps:

Step 1:

Go to this page: **www.TopMauiBook.com**.

Step 2:

Enter the validation code **090807** to claim your gift membership.

Printed in the United States
107862LV00001B/13/A

9 780975 263143